SELMA EVANS

ADHD

RAISING AN EXPLOSIVE CHILD

GUIDEBOOK FOR PARENTS TO HELP CHILDREN SELF-REGULATE, BUILD SOCIAL SKILLS, FOCUS, ORGANISE AND GAIN CONFIDENCE

ISBN: 979-12-81498-09-9

TABLE OF CONTENTS

INTRODUCTION

Raising a child with ADHD or attention deficit-hyperactivity disorder can be exhausting. It's vital for parents of these children to know that there are many different ways to parent. Regardless of how they choose to raise their child, parents should be aware of the facts.

Most children with ADHD are not hyperactive most of the time. However, the symptoms, such as hyperactivity and impulsivity, can be quite demanding and difficult for parents, teachers, and children to manage.

There are some parents who see raising a child with ADHD as being more of a challenge than parenting without this diagnosis. Some people see ADHD as a disability, and they see it as their role as parents to compensate for the disability. The child may benefit from medication and therapy. However, the child will never be "cured."

ADHD is an extremely common disorder, and it can affect any child at any time. Parents need to raise their children with guidance that fits their family values and beliefs. Parents of children with ADHD should always try to parent without prejudice or judgment of other parenting styles; there are many different options available for parents to choose from. If raised correctly, children with ADHD can become successful members of society.

This book is based on the present-day research available on ADHD. It focuses on research gaps and asks questions about certain aspects of ADHD. This book is a practical guide to raising children with ADHD, for parents who want to improve their understanding of how they can help their children learn to cope with their disorder.

Parents play an important role in the development of their child's behavior. Proper parenting can positively affect a child's behavior. However, the stress that comes with raising a child with attention deficit hyperactivity disorder can make it difficult for parents. The social stigma associated with raising children with ADHD can be emotionally toxic for parents. Parents may feel that they are failing to live up to their parental duties and responsibilities. Thus, the child's behavior is likely to be affected by this stress.

Many people believe that raising a child with ADHD means raising a child who suffers from this disorder and therefore must be taught to cope with whatever problems they might face. But the idea of first identifying the child's problems and then teaching them about coping is an outdated concept that does not take into account the strengths of the child. A child with ADHD does not need to be told how to cope with his or her behavior. Children with ADHD do not learn how to cope with their emotions; they learn how to manage them. All of us, including children with ADHD, learn by trial and error. To teach children coping skills is tantamount to telling them what is wrong with them and what they must do instead of allowing them to discover new ways to manage their issues through trial and error.

One of the biggest myths is that children with ADHD are impulsive. Research shows that children with ADHD are more likely to use thought processes of avoidance rather than impulsivity. Many parents are misinformed about their children's hyperactivity. A child with ADHD may be "hyper" because he or she is actually learning how to overcome the challenges of moving around in a new setting, sitting still for extended periods of time, or controlling impulses. When a family first begins raising a child with ADHD, they often believe that this disorder will affect every aspect of the child's life. However, this is not always true.

It is true that a child with ADHD may have difficulty learning in school, but the child's behavior in school does not necessarily affect his or her behavior outside of it. When a child with ADHD faces difficult situations at school, he or she may display difficulty coping. In other situations, the child will exhibit prosocial behavior. This demonstrates that all children with ADHD can be happy and successful members of society if they are raised correctly. With proper parenting, all children can develop into successful adults who are capable of operating effectively within society.

All parents of ADHD children need to remember that there is no one right way to parent, and every child deserves the best care and attention.

PART 1 - UNDERSTANDING ADHD IN CHILDREN

CHAPTER 1: EXPLORING ADHD: UNDERSTANDING THE DISORDER AND ITS IMPACT

ADHD is a condition affecting behavior, mood, and executive functions. Simply put, people with ADHD have a constant need for stimuli. Outgoing, reckless, and restless behavior is mainly seen in young children. ADHD can be diagnosed in adults as well, though it takes much longer for the symptoms to surface.

ADHD is not a disease but a disorder of brain wiring. ADHD is genetic and hereditary. It is caused by the way different areas of the brain communicate with each other. Sections of the brain associated with behavior, emotion, and executive functions such as planning and organizing do not communicate well with each other. Rather, these sections of the brain work independently from each other.

The condition is more prevalent in boys than girls. It is also more prevalent in children whose parents or relatives have ADHD or show symptoms of ADHD. It is said that 20% of adults living in the US have ADHD.

ADHD is a neurological condition characterized by a lack of control in the presence of overwhelming stress. Individuals with ADHD have a hard time with tasks that require strict adherence to rules. High levels of external input, such as excessive noise and movement, can overwhelm the ADHD brain, resulting in behavioral outbursts and irritability. Many children with ADHD prefer noise and chaos to deep, quiet thought or reading.

There are three types of ADHD:

1. *Predominantly Inattentive Type*

People with the predominantly inattentive type of ADHD may be very disorganized and forgetful and may frequently lose things and misplace them. When they do remember things, they tend not to hold on to them long. They can be easily distracted, even by small noises or faces that they see on television. They discover new information very slowly and need more time to finish tasks. They are impulsive, often careless, and may make poor choices.

2. *Predominantly Hyperactive/Impulsive Type*

People with the predominantly hyperactive/impulsive type of ADHD may be very impulsive and restless and may frequently interrupt others or simply get into things they shouldn't. When they remember things, they tend to hold on to them less than people with the predominantly inattentive type of ADHD. They can be easily distracted by their thoughts and can move quickly from one activity to another. They tend not to finish tasks and frequently interrupt others. They may be seen as bossy and smug by others, and they may ask many questions.

3. *Combined Type*

People with this type of ADHD may be moderately inattentive or hyperactive/impulsive, depending on which is more dominant at any one time. This brings about some very nervous behavior such as fidgeting and squirming (hyperactive) and peculiar shyness (inattentive). Often they will be both, switching back and forth between the two. They lose things easily and may be clingy with their parents. They seek out and get into trouble (hyperactive/impulsive). They can't seem to sit still and tend to move around a lot more than most people do.

Although all three types of ADHD cause problems with the areas of the brain that control attention, there is very little research on remedial medications for people with the hyperactive/impulsive type of ADHD. The medications used to treat people with the combined type of ADHD can also be used for many people with the predominantly inattentive type of ADHD, but this is not what the inventors recommend.

It is usually easier to tell if someone has an attention problem than it is to tell if they have the predominantly hyperactive/impulsive type of ADHD. However, both conditions can be very hard to treat because so many things may be triggering the symptoms, making it very hard to break out of the cycle. A person may need to be constantly distracted by outside stimuli such as loud noises, the latest news on the television, and ongoing activities such as sports or video games. The more obvious triggers that can be removed from an individual's life, the easier it will be for them to concentrate and finish tasks.

ADHD is different from dyslexia, ADD (attention deficit disorder), emotional problems or learning disabilities. This is because:

- ADHD is not an emotional problem; there is no relationship between ADHD and emotions such as in anxiety, depression, or anxiety disorders;

- ADHD is not epilepsy or a seizure disorder;

- ADHD is not aggression or oppositional behavior;

- ADHD is not caused by abuse, neglect, lack of discipline, poverty, lack of love in the home, poor parenting, too much television or video games;

- ADHD is not easily cured. If someone seems to be "cured" of their ADHD, they are simply controlling it more effectively than they were before.

- ADHD is not related to drugs, alcohol, or illegal behavior;

- ADHD does not lead to anti-social behavior.

What Causes ADHD?

There is a wide range of theories as to what causes ADHD, but the scientific consensus has linked it to a common gene that affects the prefrontal cortex development. This part of the brain is responsible for attention and impulse control and sustaining a healthy mood.

Deficiencies in this area of the brain can be found in many adults and children with ADHD.

There is also a genetic link to the condition. More than 80% of children with ADHD have a family member with the condition. The gene that causes ADHD has been found on chromosome 7. There are three major areas that can be affected by this gene:

1. Dopamine – The release of dopamine is one of the most important parts of a child's brain development. When the dopamine level is normal, attention, concentration, and memory are all enhanced. When dopamine levels are abnormal due to birth defects or damage from alcohol or drugs, it can cause problems with behavior.

2. Norepinephrine – This neurotransmitter helps in paying attention to detail. ADHD symptoms may appear when the level of this chemical in the brain is too high or too low.

3. Serotonin – This neurotransmitter is responsible for mood control in the brain. When it is out of balance in children, they can become depressed or even suicidal.

All three of these chemicals are important for healthy brain development and function. Disturbances in serotonin levels cause changes in cognition and emotional states. Low serotonin has been linked to the malfunctioning of the areas of the brain that control concentration, mood, and sleep patterns.

Scientists have found that in some people, dopamine and norepinephrine are too active in the frontal lobe. This means that they travel through the brain in abnormal patterns causing a constant need for external stimulation. As these chemicals are released, the neurons in this area of the brain become less powerful and less able to concentrate or control behavior. Stimuli, such as stress or strong emotions, can trigger strong reactions of frustration within this region of the brain. Without these chemicals, the frontal lobe is less able to control behavior and emotions.

Studies have found that less than 1% of the population has a gene that produces a deficiency in dopamine or norepinephrine, leaving most people with these chemicals constantly switched on. In some cases, this can cause ADHD due to constant overstimulation. In other cases, it has been found that these dopamine and norepinephrine levels are constantly low enough to cause serious damage to the frontal lobe of the brain.

In rare cases, these chemicals are missing entirely. These people do not experience ADHD symptoms but have a significant amount of damage to their frontal lobe, which affects their ability to think logically and concentrate on tasks.

Environmental factors can also contribute to ADHD. For example, exposure to lead during childhood has been linked to attention problems and hyperactivity later in life. Children that suffer from ADHD are more likely to have suffered from some sort of childhood trauma or abuse, which can exacerbate the symptoms of the disorder.

These days, more and more children are developing ADHD. This has been attributed to the growth in attention problems that children now experience at a younger age. TV and computer games allow children to be stimulated for longer than ever before and can cause them to become hyperactive and distracted.

As children grow, their brains are more susceptible to damage or abnormalities. Children with ADHD will often act out when they are frustrated or overwhelmed. The chemicals in the frontal lobe can build up under pressure, leading to feelings of anger and despair. The child will then break the rules in order to escape these feelings, creating a vicious circle of bad behavior.

Why Do Children Get ADHD?

As discussed above, it is believed that there is a genetic component to ADHD, meaning genetically pre-disposed individuals run a greater risk of developing the disorder than those who do not exhibit such predispositions. It has been well documented that ADHD often runs in families, and parents may exhibit traits of ADHD without actually having it themselves. If you have a relative that is diagnosed with ADHD, your children are at a higher risk of developing it as well.

While there is nothing the parent can do to prevent ADHD, it is important to take steps to reduce the risks to children. Some healthcare providers will recommend having all family members undergo genetic testing to see if any are carrying the gene for ADHD.

It is vital for parents to look out for signs of ADHD in their children as early as possible.

Risk Factors for Developing ADHD

There are certain factors that create risk, but there are no causal links between these factors and the disorder itself. It is likely that these factors only serve as triggers for individuals who already have a predisposition towards developing ADHD. Risk factors include:

Premature birth: Children born too soon and underweight have a higher likelihood of developing ADHD. Research that shows low birth weight increases the risk of ADHD by 70%.

Inactivity: Inactivity by the mother during pregnancy can increase the risk of ADHD in children because it may lead to a lack of stimulation for the fetus.

Unhealthy eating habits: Not eating enough nutritious foods, especially fats and carbohydrates, can result in low levels of dopamine and norepinephrine, which can trigger ADHD symptoms in an individual with a genetic predisposition towards the disorder.

Drugs: The use of illegal and prescription drugs among pregnant women can increase the risk of ADHD in children as they may affect the fetus' ability to regulate dopamine and norepinephrine levels.

Stress: The development of ADHD may be due to a combination of physical and psychological stressors during childhood, such as abuse or verbal humiliation by peers or siblings, family conflicts, divorce, etc. During critical periods of brain development, such as right after birth or up to the age of 3, children may be particularly vulnerable to physical and mental stressors that can trigger the development of ADHD.

Individuals who were abused as children are also more likely to develop impulse control disorders such as substance abuse problems later in life.

Brain damage: This can include brain injuries during birth or accidents at any point of one's life, or poisoning by pollutants in the environment, food, or water.

Alcohol abuse: There is a direct link between alcohol abuse and ADHD symptoms due to the damaging effects of alcohol on developing brain cells.

Environmental toxins: Exposure to toxins in the environment can trigger ADHD. These include lead, mercury, arsenic, and other pollutants. These can contribute to reduced brain volume among people with ADHD or can act as triggers for those with a genetic predisposition towards the disorder.

Outcomes of infections: Infections like meningitis or encephalitis during critical phases of brain development may trigger ADHD symptoms by causing damage to developing neurons that control concentration and behavior.

Poverty: Children who live in poverty are at high risk of developing ADHD because their brains do not always receive the stimulation they need to develop properly.

Sleep deprivation: Lack of sleep can trigger ADHD symptoms by altering levels of dopamine and norepinephrine.

High maternal stress: High stress during pregnancy can lead to children who are more sensitive to sensory stimulation (light, sound, smell, touch) and less likely to sleep well at night if they are placed in a new environment.

Statistics Regarding Children with ADHD

It is estimated that nearly 3% of children between the ages of 4 and 17 years old, or about 4.4 million children in the United States, have been diagnosed with ADHD. ADHD affects both boys and girls equally until adolescence. After age 12, more boys are diagnosed with ADHD than girls. Adults have an equal number of ADHD diagnoses as children.

In the United States, as many as 5% of children with ADHD are thought to have no family history of the disorder. In other parts of the world, one out of every seven children is diagnosed with ADHD.

It is not clear what causes some people to have more severe symptoms than others. Some believe that genetics may play a role, while others believe that environmental factors may be a more important factor. Studies have shown that there is a lot of correlation between ADHD and poverty, and certain psychological characteristics such as parent-child conflict and poor parental relationships. Of the children who have ADHD, approximately 77% live in households with incomes below $50,000 per year (US), and they also tend to be more withdrawn and aggressive than their peers. Children with the disorder are also more likely to miss school or receive lower grades.

Research suggests that individuals with ADHD may be at increased risk of developing substance abuse problems later in life due to poor impulse control caused by hyperactivity or impulsivity. About 40% of individuals with ADHD also struggle with substance abuse problems. Studies have shown that about 80% of people with untreated ADHD use drugs during their lifetime, while about 90% of adults diagnosed with ADHD were heavy alcohol users during early adulthood. Twenty-seven percent of those with untreated ADHD abuse illegal substances, while 30% of adults with untreated ADHD abuse legal substances like tobacco.

Currently, approximately 65% of children diagnosed with ADHD are treated for the disorder when they are younger than six years old. Preschool-aged children who continue to experience symptoms of ADHD after they receive treatment may need more intense treatment or may need to receive different types of treatments depending on the severity of their symptoms. Children who were diagnosed with ADHD between ages 3 and 6 and did not take medications were more likely to have poorer school results, higher levels of emotional symptoms, and poorer social relations later in life than those who took medication for their symptoms during this time period. Individuals with ADHD can still lead happy, successful, and productive lives with proper treatment. About 75% of individuals diagnosed with ADHD were able to obtain a high school diploma or GED. Approximately 70% of individuals with ADHD obtain at least an associate's degree or higher, while 60% obtain some type of college education. Individuals that suffer from ADHD are also more likely to work in unskilled labor occupations or in jobs that do not require advanced degrees or special licenses.

On average, individuals with ADHD earn $10,000 less per year than adults without the disorder for their entire adult life. For individuals with extreme cases of ADHD (i.e., those who cannot stay focused or pay attention for more than two minutes at a time), there is a 50% chance that they will be unemployed by the time they reach their 40s.

Individuals with ADHD may also experience reduced quality of life and higher rates of divorce, and children that suffer from ADHD are three times more likely to develop conduct and emotional disorders as adults than those without the disorder. The life expectancy of an individual with ADHD is the same as that of the general population.

CHAPTER 2: WHAT ARE THE SIGNS OF ADHD IN CHILDREN?

ADHD is a neurological condition. Symptoms depend on what part of the brain is impacted by the disorder. The signs of ADHD can appear at any age, even before birth. Suppose the unborn child's movement patterns are abnormal. This could be an indication that he or she may have an attention disorder later in life because abnormal movement patterns are often associated with chemical imbalances in the brain.

The symptoms of ADHD can vary from child to child, even if they have the same diagnosis. There are children that will not experience all of the symptoms of the disorder. The seriousness of symptoms depends on how long a person has been diagnosed with ADHD and what medications they are taking. Children with ADHD can have a harder time controlling their impulses than adults with the disorder, which can result in problems at home and at school.

It's normal for a child's behavior to change as he or she grows up. A person may seem fine during elementary school but suddenly begin having problems in middle or high school. This may be due to the case that they are being challenged more at school or have reached puberty and are dealing with new, changing hormones. As teens become adults, their ADHD symptoms may become more pronounced.

Early diagnosis is important for children with ADHD so they can be treated as early as possible.

Behavioral Symptoms

Behavioral symptoms are often the first thing that is noticed by parents, teachers, and other caregivers. These behaviors are not always constant or obvious to everyone, but they can be very noticeable. The more of these behaviors a child exhibits, the more likely it is that he or she will be diagnosed with ADHD.

More than 70% of children with ADHD experience inattentiveness at some time during the day. Not paying attention, not hearing what is being said, or not paying attention to schoolwork are all signs that a child may have ADHD. Oftentimes, these symptoms are accompanied by hyperactivity and impulsivity, which makes them even more difficult for teachers to deal with. If these symptoms are also combined with significant impulsiveness and hyperactivity, they may begin to adversely impact the child's ability to function socially.

Children that suffer from ADHD have difficulty staying on task. They may not pay attention for extended periods of time, and may be easily bored. These behaviors may show up as constant disobedience at home or school that can quickly escalate into major problems. Children with ADHD often struggle with organization or planning. These children also tend to act impulsively, which can cause problems for caregivers because they do not want to punish the child all the time. However, if left unchecked, these behaviors will overtake their entire life. ADHD can be treated early in life so that children with ADHD learn how to organize themselves and plan in advance in the future.

Behavioral symptoms are often associated with behavior problems at home and school. Children that struggle with ADHD often exhibit excessive behavior when upset or overwhelmed by frustration. They often tend to act out violently or destructively to release feelings of anxiety. These destructive behaviors cause problems for parents and teachers.

Cognitive Symptoms

Cognitive symptoms of ADHD often show up as problems with memory, organization, focus, attention, and comprehension. These are skills that are essential for everyday learning because they allow a child to acquire new information and retain it long enough to use later. These symptoms may include having trouble paying attention. Difficulty with the organization of thoughts is also another symptom, which makes it harder to plan and complete tasks. These symptoms may appear in different ways, such as having trouble remembering names or facts or having trouble understanding new concepts. This is sometimes referred to as executive function issues because these areas of an individual's brain help them to plan, organize, and complete tasks.

Cognitive symptoms of ADHD are often a result of a chemical imbalance in the brain. The more impulsive a child is, the more likely it is that their executive function problems are caused by ADHD. This can get worse as they get older because as they become adults, their brains become tied into cycles that make them constantly overreact to certain situations.

Visual Symptoms

Children that suffer from ADHD have a hard time focusing on visual things. They find it difficult to make visual concepts or shapes in their mind and often have a hard time describing what they see to others. This is often seen as a problem with visual-motor integration. The visual area of the brain is often thought to be connected to motor skills and movements, but some studies have shown that grown adults with ADHD have issues integrating the visual and motor areas of the brain. This area of the brain is thought to help people learn how to plan movements and execute them effectively. However, because these two areas are linked, issues with visual-motor integration may also affect the ability to plan movements.

Emotional Symptoms

Emotional symptoms of ADHD often come in the form of irritability, frustration, and intolerance. ADHD can cause a child to feel extreme emotions, and their lack of ability to cope with challenges can cause their anger to build up. These feelings can quickly become explosive and send a child into a meltdown in which he or she may throw objects, hit someone, or start screaming and crying. These symptoms can be a problem at home, at school, and with siblings.

A child with ADHD may have a hard time controlling their emotions, and this is another symptom that may show up as outbursts of anger. Children with ADHD often have trouble controlling their impulses and not acting on them. In these situations, the child's frustration becomes intense as he or she feels as though they are being controlled by their hormones or emotions.

Kids with ADHD may feel moodier than other children. A child that is impulsive may also end up getting into trouble with the law because their impulsiveness makes them act rashly rather than planning ahead.

Social Symptoms

Social symptoms may be the most difficult to understand because ADHD does not cause people to have a problem with being social. Instead, it causes them to have trouble interacting effectively. These behaviors can be seen in children who have ADHD, but they are more obvious in adults who have the disorder. It is common for children that suffer from ADHD to get into trouble at school or with other kids because of their inability to stop talking or invading other people's space. Adults with ADHD may simply not be able to understand what others are saying or feeling. They often experience social withdrawal, which makes it harder for them to find friends and maintain relationships.

Neurological Symptoms

Neurological symptoms are the least common symptoms that are seen in children with ADHD. One of these symptoms is tics. Tics are involuntary actions that may take the form of moving the eyes around, making facial expressions, or making noises now and then. These tics are often the result of an overload of dopamine in the brain's system. The third neurological symptom is distractibility or stimulus-seeking behavior, which may cause a child to be easily distracted by things that are usually not distracting for most other people. Another symptom may include a delayed reaction time to stimuli. This delay is caused by the processor in a person's brain being unable to work at a quick enough speed to keep up with the rest of their body.

Medical Symptoms

Medical symptoms are rare in children who have ADHD. These symptoms may include food allergies or intolerances, stomach pain, and frequent headaches.

Children with ADHD may also be more prone to other illnesses because they often have a hard time following rules and might not follow proper hygiene routines. They may also have trouble eating well because their impulsivity makes it harder for them to sit still long enough for meals.

Another medical symptom is sleep deprivation or sleep problems. While it is common for children with ADHD to have trouble falling asleep, a child who is having a sleep problem may also feel more tired and stressed out during the day because of it, which creates a vicious circle of symptoms.

Children with ADHD may also experience problems urinating due to the impulsive nature of the disorder, which can lead to frequent bladder infections. These symptoms may continue throughout life.

Interpersonal Symptoms

Interpersonal symptoms of ADHD can cause children to have a hard time interacting with others. This may be the result of the impulsiveness of the disorder, or it may be due to a lack of proper communication skills. Children that suffer from ADHD may find it hard to communicate their needs and wants, and this can make them appear self-centered and immature. The disorder can also make them unable to give and take criticism well. This can make it difficult for a child with ADHD to build relationships with other children and their parents.

Children who have ADHD may also be more vulnerable to bullying because of the impulsiveness associated with the disorder. Because impulsivity controls the child, he or she may find it hard to stop their impulses from causing trouble between them and others around them.

Over 60% of children with ADHD will continue to experience symptoms as adults because the disorder often goes undiagnosed and untreated. While this can make it harder for them to find and keep a job, it does not mean that they cannot go on to live happy and healthy lives.

Children who have ADHD can learn ways to cope with their symptoms through special education programs, medication, or social programs. These measures will help them interact with others more effectively and form friendships.

Children who have ADHD may experience different degrees of the disorder throughout their lives. When a child diagnosed with ADHD at age 7 experiences an episode at age 23, the severity of the symptoms may be greater or less than those they experienced as a child. Whether this occurs due to environmental factors or genetics is unclear, but it is something parents should keep in mind when planning for their children's future education and healthcare.

CHAPTER 3: IDENTIFYING ADHD DIFFERENCES BETWEEN GIRLS AND BOYS

E arly diagnosis of ADHD in children can be difficult. These difficulties are often due to gender stereotypes, limited research on the subject, and the fact that some children's symptoms may not be obvious until they reach puberty. ADHD is almost three times more common in boys than it is in girls. However, some studies estimate that more than 20 percent of girls have ADHD. In boys, ADHD is more likely to be diagnosed in preschool when it often presents as hyperactivity. But in girls, ADHD can show up anywhere from infancy through to adolescence.

The diagnostic criteria for ADHD are similar for both males and females, but there are some slight differences in the behaviors that are considered with each gender. Schools, teachers, and parents often differ in their opinions of what behaviors are appropriate for these children. It's important that parents and teachers learn to recognize ADHD in males and females alike, as the symptoms of ADHD may not be as obvious in girls as they are in boys.

Studies show that girls with ADHD may be more likely to also suffer from oppositional defiant disorder (ODD) or anxiety. They may be less impulsive and more likely to internalize their emotions and worries compared to boys with ADHD.

The first step in determining whether your child has ADHD is to consult your physician, who will suggest further testing if he or she feels it's necessary. It is very important that your physician rule out other medical conditions that may cause similar symptoms to ADHD.

Distinct behavioral signs of ADHD in girls

- Girls with ADHD may display more anxious behavior than boys. Behaviors associated with anxiety can cause problems at home or in school.

- Girls often feel like they are losing control over their lives and become frustrated easily. They may feel like no one understands them or what they are going through, which can make it harder for them to control their behavior.

- Girls can be more rebellious than boys. They may be intolerant of criticism and often become impatient with rules.

- Girls can be prone to frustration and tend to feel bored with repetitive tasks. They may act out when they are around too many people or when they are unable to concentrate on one activity for an extended period of time. Sometimes, their self-esteem will plummet, which makes it harder for them to control their behavior.

- Girls may feel anxious and frustrated with school and therefore begin to display troubling behavior. They may not be able to focus at all and will sometimes perform poorly on tests and assignments. This lack of concentration can make them feel like they are incapable of advancing academically.

- Girls often lack self-esteem and often deal with depression and anxiety. They may be unable to understand the negative effects their behavior has on others. They may also become very cynical about their chances of success in life, which can make it harder for them to improve how they feel about themselves.

- Girls with ADHD tend to be more impulsive than boys, especially when it comes to their social connections. They often have a hard time reading other people's feelings and emotions accurately. Even when they do understand how other people feel, they struggle to control their behavior in the situation. They may find it easier to speak to a friend than they do to a teacher or adult.

- Girls with ADHD often feel like they are not loved or needed by anyone and that their place in society is insignificant. They can be very sensitive and may overreact when someone is criticizing them.

- Girls with ADHD often become frustrated with their schoolwork and will become agitated when they feel like they aren't learning anything.

- Girls with ADHD can develop problems around food and eating. They may binge eat unhealthy foods or even starve themselves in an effort to lose weight.

- Girls with ADHD often exhibit cognitive behavior that is similar to that of adults with the disorder.

Distinct behavioral signs of ADHD in boys

- Boys with ADHD often display more impulsive behavior than typical children. They may become irritated or angry with those around them and can react negatively to criticism.

- Boys often make decisions on the spur of the moment. They may not be able to control their emotions, especially when they feel threatened or emotionally frustrated. This can lead to outbursts of anger that can cause a lot of damage, both emotionally and physically.

- Boys with ADHD often have problems sleeping. This can cause them to act out during the day or fight with their parents over bedtime. This behavior can cause relationship problems, as well as problems in school performance.

- Boys with ADHD tend to be more reckless than other boys, and they also may display more aggressive behavior than girls with ADHD. This behavior can cause emotional distress for the child, as well as those around him or her.

- Boys with ADHD may not be able to keep up with physical activity, and this can cause them to feel frustrated and lose interest in sports. They may also have problems finding a sport or activity that keeps them engaged for an extended period of time because they get bored so easily.

- Boys may have more trouble controlling their emotions than girls do. They may cry more often and become upset when they don't get what they want.

- Boys often feel angry or frustrated that they can't do what others are doing. They may feel like they are not as competent as others, which can cause emotional problems and conflict within their social groups.

- Boys with ADHD are more likely to experience problems with violence or aggression than other children. They may hurt themselves, get into fights, get in trouble at school, get in trouble with the law, or act out sexually.

- Boys may not develop the social skills that they need in order to get along with others. They may even begin to display bullying behavior that is meant to make them feel powerful or aggressive.

- Boys may be less motivated than other children their age, and this can lead them to act out when they don't feel like putting in much effort. They may become impulsive, which makes it difficult for them to exercise self-control.

- Boys may have problems with their sleep and eat more than they need, causing unhealthy weight gain.

Things you can do if your child is suffering from ADHD

If you believe that your child has ADHD, talk with your child's pediatrician. The doctor may refer you to a mental health or behavioral therapist who can perform a proper diagnosis and help develop a treatment plan.

Although medication may be a good option for many parents, the doctor should always recommend a multidisciplinary approach to treat your child. This includes a coordinated team of professionals who can help your child learn how to control his or her behavior. The family should also participate in group therapy sessions in order to build strong social relationships and improve their mental health overall.

If the treatment methods don't work for you, you may wish to explore other options. However, you should discuss each option with your doctor and a mental health professional prior to beginning any new treatment method.

It is important to remember that untreated ADHD will continue to cause problems in your child's life. These problems can worsen as your child gets older. It is critical that you seek treatment for your child before their condition worsens.

Kids with ADHD often feel anxious about their living arrangements, which leads them to feel confused and upset. They may be unsure about where they belong or who they are. Therapy can help them learn how to cope with their feelings in healthy ways, rather than resorting to unhealthy behaviors.

If you are anxious about your child's behavior, talk with your pediatrician or mental health professional about their progress. This way, you can make sure that they are on the right path to living a full and healthy life.

PART 2 - MANAGEMENT OF ADHD AT HOME

CHAPTER 4: EFFECTS OF A CHILD WITH ADHD ON THE DYNAMICS OF FAMILY LIFE

I f your child has ADHD, you may struggle to set appropriate boundaries for behavior. You may feel you are not respected or taken seriously by your child. You may feel more challenged than other parents when it comes to teaching and managing behavior at home.

You might be trying to do too much yourself, and you might be inadvertently reinforcing negative behaviors by trying to do too much for your child. You may also be discouraged about how your spouse and other children seem to enable the child's misbehavior and lack of responsibility. You may feel unappreciated and unacknowledged.

What's more, once the novelty of the "new baby" wears off, other children in the family begin to feel neglected and resentful and sometimes hostile toward your child.

As a result of their child's difficulties, parents often find themselves overwhelmed by feelings of guilt, anger, or depression. And because your child's behavior usually affects the entire family, you may feel plagued by guilt or bitterness toward your spouse or other children. You may feel incredibly frustrated and resentful when you try to set boundaries, and the child doesn't understand why he can't have everything he wants.

Many parents feel discouraged and hopeless about their child's long-term prospects. They may feel as if they have tried everything to be successful as a parent, spouse, and family member. Such feelings are understandable.

It is acceptable to expect that the more problems you have been having with your child and the more complex and challenging the situation has become, the harder it will be to make changes or see results, but changing the way you and your family function is possible and will make a significant difference in your life and the life of your child.

It is essential to be realistic about what you can do to help yourself and your family, and it is even more critical for you to consider the impact that a child with ADHD can have on a family. How is your child's behavior affecting the state of your marriage, the level of stress in your family, and your child's relationships with their siblings?

Many of the children you are raising will someday live independently. But before they do so, they will have to learn how to function successfully as part of a family. They will have to learn how to get along with others and take responsibility for their actions. In addition, they need to develop social skills that allow them to be successful in school and work relationships.

Parents who care for a child that suffers from ADHD want their children to learn how to function correctly as part of a family and as independent adults in the community. They want their children to know how to be responsible members of society, but at the same time, they may become so frustrated by a child's behavior that they give up on the idea of them ever learning how to function in a family or community. They may become adults with ADHD who never learned how to function successfully in relationships and who are too overwhelmed by anger or depression to make changes in their behavior.

Strained parent-child relationships

It is not uncommon for children that suffer from ADHD to get in trouble for their behavior, be criticized, and disciplined more frequently than their siblings. This fact alone can create stress in the relationships between parents and children. Parents of children with ADHD may feel like they are always the bad guys in the eyes of their children.

When parents find themselves in this situation, they may react by becoming angry or withdrawn even when there is little or nothing wrong with what the child has done. Such reactions may make the child feel confused and misunderstood. This can cause both parents and children to feel locked in a continuous cycle of miscommunication and reaction.

Parents who feel irritable or angry when their child misbehaves may have trouble setting limits on behavior. They may become more involved in power struggles with their child than in helping the child learn appropriate behaviors.

It is essential for parents to recognize that their feelings are normal and that they need to make a positive effort to change their behavior.

Parents can help both themselves and their child by learning ways to respond calmly and with consistency to the child's behavior. Consistently applied responses help children know what they can expect from parents even when they do not hear what they want. Consistency is also essential for teaching necessary life skills.

Most children do best when they know that their parents are available to listen to them and to be trusted by them. But negative behaviors can quickly lead to a child losing trust in their parents' ability to take care of his well-being. If this happens, it may be difficult for the parent to regain the trust lost.

For example, if a child feels that he is being ignored or treated unfairly, he may become even more defiant, angry, or upset with the world around him. The child may become increasingly self-focused or rudely intrusive toward other people's space and time—not only within the family but also in the community.

Such defiant or intrusive behavior can be particularly frustrating for parents who feel they are doing all they can to help their child adjust to the difficulties of raising him. They may feel defeated and hopeless, especially if their child is often in trouble at school or has had problems getting along with teachers, peers, friends, or playmates. Parents need to remember that, like many people with ADHD (even adults!), children with ADHD are capable of learning how to relate in positive ways with others. But if their behavior is left unsupervised and without consequences, they will always find new challenging behaviors in which they can engage. Similarly, if parents do not engage in consistent and meaningful interactions with their child, they cannot expect results.

Parents need to know what they are doing right, not only what they are doing wrong. This is essential for helping them keep their self-esteem high enough to be able to keep working with their child.

The fastest way to lose self-esteem is by reacting with anger or resentment to a child's negative behavior. Parents need to know that they are the adults in the situation. As adults, they can choose how they will respond when a child or teenager acts inappropriately or complains about the way he has been treated. A parent may, for example, decide he does not have time for his son's complaints because he needs to get dinner on the table before it gets cold. In this situation, a parent can say firmly, "That's your problem." In order to maintain consistency in the relationship, the parent may also remind him that he needs to make his bed before 8:00 a.m. The parent will continue with his conversation without blaming the child for anything. This is an example of how a parent can react quickly and firmly in a way that is consistent with what he truly intends but is not intended to convey disrespect for the child.

Parents also need to practice responding calmly and consistently to their child's behavior. If a parent becomes angry or sarcastic when a child makes a complaint about the way he is being treated, he may actually be saying, "I feel I can't trust you." The child may think the parent is angry because he thinks the child is not caring enough about himself.

If parents respond negatively to their children's complaints, they may also inadvertently convey their own feelings of anger, frustration, helplessness and resentment. This can cause confusion in the relationship and make it very hard for both children and parents to learn how to deal with one another.

Like most people, children with ADHD want to be trusted and respected. They want their parents to care about the way they feel.

Setting limits on behavior

Parents should set limits on their child's behavior that are reasonable, consistent, and age-appropriate. With the help of a qualified professional, children with ADHD can learn to accept these limits and to behave in acceptable ways. This will help both parent and child become more involved in managing the child's behavior, which will lead to better communication between them.

Parents can minimize the challenges to their own feelings by learning to see their child's challenging behaviors as manageable problems that do not reflect on the child's worth as a human being. Parents can also benefit from understanding why their child behaves in certain ways and what they can do about it. They should keep in mind that they have choices about how to respond when their child acts out, and they have a responsibility for deciding what kind of relationship they want to have with their child.

Limiting misbehavior by children with ADHD is often a challenge because it involves setting limits on behaviors that are important to parents. It may be very hard to set limits on behaviors such as hyperactivity or impulsivity, even when a child's behavior is inappropriate or troublesome. After all, the behaviors are very hard to control.

As a result of their difficulties with setting limits on their child's behavior, some parents have been known to withhold affection from the child because he misbehaves. However, doing so can make the child more defiant. Instead of withholding affection, parents need to learn how to manage difficult behaviors by using consistent responses.

Even minor misbehaviors can create problems in interpersonal relationships. Providing young children with structure and consistency at home makes it more likely that they will behave the same way at school.

Teaching appropriate behavior is essential for children with ADHD, who require boundaries that are very clear and firm. Effective discipline techniques need to be part of any program for children with ADHD. Children need to learn how to accept and follow the rules and deal with misbehaviors.

The following are some guidelines on how to deal with misbehavior:

- When you first notice the behavior, calmly let the child know what he is doing wrong.

- Talk to your child about what he is doing. Find out why he is misbehaving. Remember that his actions are not random but that they are related to his environment or personal needs or feelings. The more you can understand why your child behaves as he does, the better chance you will have of helping him change his behavior.

- In order to calm tantrums, parents should try to find out what is wrong with their child and help him or she solve the problem. This may involve helping the child learn appropriate ways of dealing with anger.

- If your child gets upset when you ask him to stop doing something, remember that you are asking them to work on changing behavior that you both want to change. This means that your child is responding in his own way and most likely wants to do what you ask, even if it upsets him at first.

- Set clear, positive limits with your child. These should be stated as what you want your child to do and not do. The more specific you are about the behavior, the clearer the message will be. Also, you will have a harder time backing down than if you had not been specific about what behavior was appropriate.

- Use timeouts or other consequences with your child when they misbehave. These will help your child learn that his behavior is unacceptable. However, rather than using them as punishments, you should use timeouts to encourage a shift in behavior with a clear message: "I want you to stop doing this."

- When you teach your child new ways of responding to misbehavior, give him support for what he is doing. Also, show him how he can use the new responses to build better behaviors.

- Be sure that you are consistent with your limits on behavior.

- Let your child know what to expect. If you are clear about what want your child to do, he will be more able to make the necessary changes in his behavior.

- Try not to get annoyed when your child does something wrong. This will help him to see that you are not upset with him about it and that he can stop doing it if he wants to.

- Treat the misbehavior as the first step toward change, rather than punishing it.

- Teach your child how to manage their own emotions about misbehavior by using self-management skills such as breathing, relaxation, taking time out to calm down, and getting closer to someone who can help them deal with anger or other feelings.

- When your child misbehaves, try to understand whether the behavior reflects their feelings. Use this understanding to help your child learn how to deal with their emotions.

- Remember that because your child is learning, he will often resist new ways of doing things. This is normal and will pass as he learns that what you want is best for him.

- Be sure to let your child know that you love them, no matter how they act.

- Let your child have an opinion on the limits you set. Do this by setting limits based on mutual agreements between parents and children.

- Remember that what you do to show that you care about your child has more power than anything else in teaching them what right and wrong behavior is.

- Remember that even bad behavior can be used as a teaching tool. It can be used as a way to teach your child that they can learn to do what you want.

- Do not yell at your children in public. Yelling can make it harder for them to respond in ways they know are right, like following directions or making good choices.

- Teach your child how to find someone who can help, like an adult, when they are upset with peers or other people.

- Teach your child how to use appropriate emotional words, like "Help me" or "I am scared." Children who learn to communicate their emotions clearly will be able to deal with them better.

- Remember that it is common for children to explore behaviors during the preschool years, even behaviors that may be wrong or hurtful. When your child makes a mistake, be sure to teach them the right way to do it.

- Try not to get pulled into power struggles with your child when they misbehave. Discuss how you want your child to act in certain situations.

-

Remember that it is common for children to act out during the preschool years. This is part of growing up, which includes learning how to sort out right from wrong.

- It is typical for children to feel sad, angry, or scared when they misbehave. This is part of growing up and learning how to deal with emotions. Teach your child the difference between appropriate feelings and inappropriate feelings (like wanting to hurt someone), and teach them to manage difficult feelings.

- Show your child you love them, even when they are hurting you or doing something wrong. This will teach them how to return the love when someone else does something for them.

- Give your child the love and support they need as they grow older. Love can help them deal with difficult feelings.

Teach your children how to deal with the world by being a good role model. Your child needs you to be consistent in your teachings about right and wrong behavior–what is allowed and what is not.

Parent Training

Parent training is one of the most effective interventions for families with ADHD children. This involves teaching parents how to create a structure for their children while allowing them to be free and enjoy childhood. The main goal of parent training is to teach parents to be more effective in parenting. Parent training systematically teaches parents the skills that they need in order to help their children become well-adjusted and independent. It also builds the relationship between parents and their children by focusing on problem-solving, which requires both sides to work together toward a common goal.

Studies have shown that parent training is successful in helping parents cope with ADHD symptoms in their children. It requires the involvement of both the parents and the children. Parents will learn positive child management strategies that will help them teach their children to become independent. Children are also encouraged to participate by expressing their feelings and concerns about what is happening in their lives. They learn to express themselves using the techniques they have learned in parent training.

Your child needs the structure of a routine in order to function effectively. For example, you could establish a family ritual each night before bedtime, such as saying prayers or making a special snack. If there are problems with this routine, speak about them with your child at regular intervals. Keep these matters in mind when you are making the daily schedule for your child.

Make sure that other people in your child's life know about these routines, such as teachers, other parents, and other caregivers. If other people know what will happen during the day or at certain times, they can be prepared for these events

You can guide your child with ADHD by teaching them to use their time wisely. This will prepare them for the future and help give them a sense of direction. Helping them initiate and set goals during their youth may also help your child overcome some of the negative aspects of their ADHD later in life. If you teach your child to set goals, they may be more positive about taking on challenges. You can also help your child by teaching them to make friends with others who have the same interests. This will help them solve problems and find common ground. It will also help them feel good about themselves because they will have someone else who understands what they are going through.

Your child needs to be allowed to spend time on their own during the day. If they have difficulty completing tasks, it may be helpful for you to step in and help them finish their work. Do not let your child with ADHD experience a sense of helplessness by not allowing them to complete important tasks at home.

It is vital for parents to make sure that their children are not feeling stressed. If their child feels defeated and overwhelmed, they may be more likely to complain about everyday situations and feel frustrated. Encourage your child to take breaks and take a step back from their day-to-day struggles. Remember that we all have times when we do not feel like doing certain things, such as waking up in the morning or going to school. These are all part of everyday life and should not be seen as failures or limitations when it comes to coping with ADHD symptoms.

Parents need to make sure they communicate well with their children. Encourage them to make their own decisions and do not let others control these choices.

Children with ADHD often request a lot of attention from their caregivers. When they need help, they might pull on parents' sleeves or interrupt what a parent is trying to do. These behaviors can cause parents to become even more frustrated by their child's behavior. During this time, it is important to stop what you are doing and pay attention to your child. If you feel too overwhelmed, try to find someone else in your household who can help by playing with your child or spending time with them while you take a few moments to destress.

If your child has ADHD, it is important not to make them feel like they are failing because of this disorder. It is very easy for these children to feel discouraged, but this will only cause more problems in the long run. It is important to be patient and understanding when it comes to your child's feelings. You can also help your child by supporting them when they make progress with their tasks. Never make your child feel terrible about their struggles with ADHD. They need love and support in all aspects of their life in order to overcome these challenges.

It is important to treat your child as an individual. Your child will be likely to succeed in life if you allow them to communicate their thoughts and feelings. It may also be good for your family to begin having actual conversations about your child's struggles with ADHD so you can learn and understand how they experience this disorder. This will help you to feel closer and more connected to your child. It will also help you to learn how to be a good support system for your child in future.

Everyone with ADHD has their own unique strengths and weaknesses. Your child will come to an understanding of ADHD as they mature. During this time, you can help your child by making sure that they are no longer feeling overwhelmed and frustrated by the difficulties associated with the disorder.

It is also very important for your child to understand that feelings and emotions can be very powerful. If your child feels overwhelmed because of the struggles associated with the disorder, they may not be able to convey their feelings properly. This may cause them to become more frustrated, and to feel as if there is something wrong with them. This will only decrease a child's self-esteem. If you see your child with ADHD becoming frustrated or overwhelmed, try to help them to take a step back and give them some time to recover.

Children with ADHD usually make the mistake of blaming themselves for their struggles, which leads them to experience a sense of hopelessness. When your child is struggling, do not allow them to feel that this is something that they cannot do anything about. If your children understand that there really is nothing wrong with them and that they will be able to cope with their symptoms as adults, they will learn how to be more accepting of themselves and others.

Distorted sibling relationships

Siblings of children with ADHD may become the target of the child's behavior. They may be teased or isolated. Siblings have a lot of influence on each other, so it is important for parents to pay attention to the "little world" that children are forming for themselves.

Many children with ADHD have siblings who do not have the disorder, so it is important for parents to learn about both types of children. Parents should learn to recognize that the siblings of a child with ADHD are not responsible for the child's behavior and therefore should not be held accountable for disciplining their brother or sister.

Parents may be able to resolve sibling conflicts by taking a proactive approach. They can sit down with the siblings and work out an agreement as to what they will and will not do, including watching TV together or going shopping together if they want to.

Some parents of children with ADHD may find that their children's siblings begin to imitate them and adopt similar challenging behaviors. Parents can help the siblings understand this by first talking about what they are doing, then asking them to stop, and finally offering them alternative behaviors.

The sibling of a child with ADHD needs to learn that he or she does not have to put up with certain behaviors from their brother or sister. Very often, siblings become accustomed to "putting up" with the behavior of their ADHD brother or sister. They may even begin to believe that the behavior is okay because everyone else seems to allow it.

Siblings can and should set limits, and need to learn that they do not have to do everything their brother or sister wants them to. They can say no, even if their sibling does not like it.

However, children need to learn not to blame their sibling with ADHD for all of the problems in their family. They can get angry and frustrated when they see how their brother or sister is treated by their parents, especially if it is different from how they are treated. Siblings can get along better if they recognize that their brother or sister did not choose to have ADHD and that he or she needs love and understanding just like anyone else.

Parents can help their children see their sibling with ADHD needs different, but still important, attention and affection. Parents can also help their children understand that it is possible for them to really enjoy their brother or sister's company and that they do not always have to be quiet and live in his or her shadow.

Sometimes parents will find that people treat one of their children differently from the other. In many cases, this is not malicious, but the non-ADHD siblings may need to learn how to be seen as an individual nonetheless. If they are always overshadowed by their ADHD brother or sister, they will need to learn how to make their presence felt.

If a child with ADHD has a sibling who is a "pleaser," the sibling may feel accountable for making sure that everything goes right for his or her brother or sister. These children can become overwhelmed easily and feel that they have to take on the responsibility for everything in the family so as not to burden their parents.

Parents should give the siblings of the child with ADHD the opportunity to express any negative feelings they have about this disorder. They should not be afraid to talk about how things are affecting them. It can be helpful for children to understand what it is like for their sibling to struggle with this disorder.

It can be difficult for the siblings to understand that his or her brother or sister will never be able to perform like they are capable of doing. They may try to help their sibling in every way possible, but they may add to the sibling's problems by pushing them too hard, particularly in the areas of academia and sports.

Children with ADHD will usually need extra help and attention than the other children in their families, but this does not mean that they are more important to the family. It does mean that more of the family's resources will need to be devoted to helping them focus attention and learning how to behave appropriately.

It is important for parents of a child with ADHD to make sure that their siblings understand that they are not responsible for solving these problems. One of the best ways for this understanding to be reached is for all of the siblings who are living at home at the time of diagnosis to meet with a mental health professional who specializes in working with families of children with ADHD. This professional will be able to help the siblings understand that they are not responsible for fixing this problem and that it is not their place to try to fix it themselves or give advice about their brother or sister's behavior.

This can be a demanding situation for everyone involved, but it is crucial for parents to relax their expectations so they do not cause more problems. Parents should try to stay at the same level of expectations as they would have had if their child were being raised without ADHD.

Parents need to be understanding of their children's feelings so they can learn what they are going through. By being open about the sibling's feelings, the rest of the family can give them support so they do not have to feel so alone in their struggles. An older child with ADHD may feel lonely and isolated from people who do not have this disorder.

The family of a child that suffers from ADHD will need to be careful about how much information about this disorder they share with their other children. This news can make it feel like someone in the family is being singled out or blamed for causing all problems. They may conclude that because someone in the family has ADHD, no one will like them. Although this is certainly not true, there are still people who do not understand this disorder well enough to know that it sometimes has nothing to do with how someone acts.

Because of this, it is often helpful if the family only shares the information about ADHD as necessary. This will help to decrease the number of problems that other siblings living at home are likely to have.

CHAPTER 5: ESTABLISHING SERENITY WITHIN YOUR HOUSEHOLD

Children with ADHD can create a lot of stress and anxiety for families. The child's symptoms can cause disruptions at home and can leave families feeling unhappy and stressed out. They may be tense, irritable, and frustrated. Parenting children with ADHD can be emotionally and physically demanding, even though ADHD symptoms will lessen as the child ages. Parents need to be prepared for the emotional and physical demands of children with ADHD. This chapter discusses how parents can create calm and order at home and prevent stress from affecting them and their children.

ADHD does affect not only the child but also the entire family unit. Parents and siblings suffer emotional and physical stress from the symptoms of ADHD, such as disappointment, resentment, anger, and frustration. The parents need to create calm at home for their child with ADHD and their other children. This helps keep the family unit happy and functioning well, which will positively affect the child.

Parents also need to create calm at home to remain in control of their own emotions and behavior, so they can deal with their child's ADHD in a calm, effective way. Children with ADHD often ask for multiple things from their parents. They may interrupt parents when they are in the middle of talking to another adult, or in the middle of watching television. Often they may run around the house screaming or yell at their parents for not paying enough attention to them. Children with ADHD may jump up and down on furniture, bounce balls against walls, bang things together, throw toys across rooms, and slam doors. They may ask for multiple snacks throughout the day. They may want their parents and siblings to entertain them, while the parents may be tired and not in the mood to play. Children with ADHD demand a lot of attention from their parents, siblings, relatives, and the entire family unit.

The Importance of Stress Management Strategies for Parents

Children with ADHD may become increasingly unruly and unpleasant as the demands of everyday life start to pile up. To cope with these situations, parents can try to develop a sense of humor. They should remember that laughter will get them through many stressful episodes. To get the most from humor, parents should learn to be able to laugh at themselves.

Parents can learn to manage their stress by learning three skills:

Learning to think strategically about their own needs vs. the child's needs.

It is important for parents to learn to prioritize their own needs rather than those of their child with ADHD. They can also learn to stay cool under pressure by refusing to be ruled by emotions, such as fear, anger, frustration, self-criticism, or guilt.

Learning that they do not need to control everything in the home environment in order for them and their children to feel happy and well adjusted.

Being in control is very important for parents with ADHD. However, they do not need to be able to fix every problem and maintain a strict schedule in order for them and their children to feel happy and well adjusted.

Learning that the most important measure of success is feeling good about themselves, rather than measuring their children's performance according to how well they perform compared to other children.

Another strategy for parents to use is to develop an active relaxation program that includes self-soothing activities such as reading, listening to music, or taking a warm bath.

Parents can also practice deep breathing in order to reduce stress levels. Deep breathing exercises are a simple and effective way to relax in a stressful situation. Parents can also learn to prevent their stress from getting out of control by developing a positive coping style and learning how they can deal effectively with ADHD symptoms in their children without becoming angry or frustrated.

Children whose parents are able to manage stress better are more likely to be successful with ADHD management because they will be able to provide better guidance and support than parents who are not able to cope with their stress effectively.

Relaxation exercises

Relaxation exercises are a very effective way for parents to deal with stress. The exercises can help parents remain calm and in control in situations that may be a challenge for them.

When parents learn to relax their bodies, they will provide more support for their children. Similarly, children with ADHD often have trouble focusing on tasks and paying attention when they feel stressed or anxious about something, so it is important for them to learn how to use deep breathing and other relaxation techniques when they become anxious or upset.

Relaxation exercises can help relieve stress and tension in a situation that is making someone angry. Angry children may feel even angrier because they are disappointed by their inability to calm down. They may be angry with themselves because they know that they should not be reacting excessively or losing composure, but at the same time, they cannot control how they feel.

By learning how to use relaxation exercises, people can calm themselves down and make better decisions.

Studies have shown that relaxation exercises are very helpful for children with ADHD. It has been found that the more time parents spend meditating, the more their children will improve in school. Studies also indicate that mindfulness meditation may help people deal better with the stresses of everyday life.

Relaxation exercises are very easy to learn and can be done by anyone.

Meditation

Meditation can be helpful to parents of children with ADHD because it enables them to relax and manage their emotions. Because parents may feel very frustrated and angry, they need to find a way to calm themselves down so they can deal more effectively with their children.

Meditation has been shown to help both children and adults deal with stress. It can lower blood pressure, raise the level of endorphins (the body's natural painkillers), and relax muscles. It is also a way to relieve pain and even to help people sleep.

The benefits of meditation can be felt for a long time after the session is over. It helps people develop better ways to handle stressful situations, and helps them make better decisions.

Anyone can learn how to meditate by finding a quiet place and listening to calming music or sounds such as the ocean, a bird singing outside your house, or simply by listening to your breathing for several minutes. To help you concentrate, you can focus on what you hear or stare at a candle for fifteen minutes.

How to meditate:

- Choose a quiet place to do the exercise.

- Turn off any devices that may be making noise, such as radios and cell phones.

- Try to eliminate any sources of light, such as lamps and ceiling lights.

- Wear loose clothing and sit on a comfortable surface.

- Begin by establishing a few minutes of deep breathing and then gradually letting distractions and stressors fade away until the body feels relaxed. If you begin to feel stressed or agitated, bring your attention back to your breathing.

- Try to avoid judgment during this exercise, both internal and external.

- Try to avoid being too critical of past mistakes or thoughts that might pop into your mind.

- Let thoughts come and go without becoming fixated on them.

Meditation is for everyone! It is a great way to help anyone who tries it become more productive, less stressed, and much happier. Meditation also promotes better health because it helps people with ADHD manage their symptoms more effectively.

People who meditate regularly tend to respond better to stressful situations than people who do not meditate. By learning how to meditate, parents can help their children handle angry feelings more effectively. Parents who meditate regularly can also provide more active and solid support to their children because they will better deal with their stress and anger.

Getting a good night's sleep

Studies have shown that getting a good night's sleep is essential for healthy living, and that lack of sleep can cause a wide range of physical and mental problems. It is essential to get a good amount of sleep, on average around 8-9 hours a night.

Sleep deprivation can cause several issues with the brain. The pituitary gland dictates whether or not you feel awake or tired. If you are sleep-deprived, your body will produce more cortisol, which affects the amount of testosterone in the body. More testosterone produces more energy, and less cortisol means that you will feel less anxious during stressful situations.

If a person does not get enough sleep, he may find it difficult to concentrate on tasks, and his mood might be more irritable due to an increase in stress hormones such as cortisol and adrenaline. One study showed that a lack of sleep caused a significant increase in appetite for people who were not obese. People who were obese showed little change in appetite. However, those who were not obese showed increases in their weight as a result of the lack of sleep.

There are many ways to help you to get better quality sleep. These include:

- Sleeping on a pillow that supports your head and neck and makes it easier for you to turn over and bend your legs.

- Using sound-soothing products such as white noise can help you fall asleep at night.

- Avoiding bright lights before you go to bed because bright lights will make your body think it is still daytime.

- Avoiding caffeinated drinks late at night because it will make it harder for you to fall asleep.

- Avoiding eating too much sugar or fatty foods before going to bed. Eating a high carbohydrate meal before going to sleep can cause blood sugar levels to drop abruptly, which can wake you up at night.

- Relaxing activities such as a warm shower, a good book, a warm bath, music, meditation, and deep breathing can also help you sleep. If you are feeling stressed or restless, try to relax your mind and body before going to sleep.

Avoid doing demanding tasks such as note-taking just before bedtime because this can keep your mind awake and hinder you from falling asleep easily.

Relax your mind by thinking of nature or picturing a place that makes you feel at peace. Do this for five minutes when it is time for you to go to sleep.

It is also a nice idea to try and do some kind of physical activity, even if it is just walking after dinner. The exercise will help tire your muscles and you will fall asleep more easily at night. If you are able to get in some form of exercise each day, you will sleep better at night

Parents who have slept properly will be more productive during the day. Parents can help their children by having healthy sleeping habits.

Respite

Another way to help parents and children with ADHD is through respite services. Respite allows parents to find a place where they can take their child for a short period of time, just long enough for them to have some time to themselves. Parents are often very stressed out by the daily care they have to provide for their children, but just because they are stressed does not mean that they do not love their children or are terrible parents. As difficult as it might be, parents need to learn how to prioritize their own needs so they can give everything that is needed to their children. Respite is a great way to help the family as a whole learn how to incorporate relaxation into their lives. Overtired parents will not be as effective as those who have been given a little "time out."

The respite service provider should be familiar with the child's needs and the way that ADHD affects the family. They will then be able to develop a plan together that helps them manage situations better in the future.

There are many options available for respite care. These can include daycare programs, community centers, family members, and professional caregivers hired privately by the parent or through state funding.

Parents who have children with ADHD should not be afraid to ask for assistance when they need it. There are many resources available, and it can benefit everyone involved if parents take advantage of them.

Finding a Support Group and Getting Therapy

Many parents have said that they feel better when they go to therapy because they are with other parents who understand what they are going through. These parents learn how to handle sticky situations in the home and gain the strength and courage to deal with them when they arise. They learn to express their anger therapeutically, not toward each other, but toward the disorder affecting everyone involved. They can talk out loud about things that bother them without being told that they are wrong or being blamed for anything. They can also talk about ways to improve the home environment and how to make changes.

Parents who go to therapy will gain a better understanding of how ADHD affects everyone in their family. They can learn some parenting techniques and discover things about themselves as individuals and parents. A therapist can also help the family get more organized. Everyone in the home can learn to let go of things that are not working, and they can work together to make developments that will benefit everyone.

A therapist can also help the family deal more effectively with their child's behavior. Parents can learn that they are not responsible for their children's behavior, and they will be able to understand that their child is not doing it just to get them upset.

Therapy provides parents with new coping skills as well as encouragement. They will learn how to deal with situations in more productive ways. They will learn how to cope with stressful situations better by remembering that everyone is involved, not just one person who has difficulty. They will also learn techniques for dealing more effectively with the behaviors of others around them.

Sometimes parents may require medication to cope with the challenges of parenting a child with ADHD. A therapist can help parents find the appropriate medication that will allow them to control their feelings, cope more effectively, and manage their behavior better. The therapist can also provide information about how medications work as well as which ones are most appropriate for each individual.

Children with ADHD face many challenges, and it is up to them and their parents to find ways to deal with them so that everyone can be successful in life. Some parents think that they are alone in this because they don't think that any other parents could possibly understand everything that they are going through. They give up before even trying because they feel like no one has ever gone through anything like this before. The fact is that there are millions of other people who have gone through what you are going through. They get through it and get better.

Making changes in the home environment can be difficult, but doing so can bring about many benefits in the future. Parents should seek therapy for themselves as well as their children in order to cope with the challenges that they are facing. They need to know that they are not alone. The more support that parents get, the better off everyone will be.

Routines and Structure

Having a routine for your child's day can be very beneficial to his or her well-being. It helps your child to feel secure because he or she knows what is expected of them every day at the same time. For example, if your children take a nap every day at two o'clock, they will associate that time with feeling tired and going to sleep on their own.

It is also important to have structure in the home. Each family member needs to have a certain amount of responsibility, and they need to know what their role in the family is. All family members should feel responsible for what goes on in the home, and each person needs to grasp where he or she fits in to the structure of things.

Children can become very frustrated if they do not know where they stand in the family. If they know that their mother expects them to help her around the house, but their father does not, then this can cause a problem. If a child feels that he or she is being treated unfairly, this can lead to problems at school and home because the child may be angry and feel that he or she has been mistreated. The child's behavior may also stress out his or her parents and affect their ability to enjoy life.

Creating good routines will also help all family members to be better prepared for dealing with children with ADHD because you will all know what to expect. If you know what things are typically done at what time, you won't be too surprised when your child does (or does not) do something each day. This will help everyone feel happy and confident about life.

Children need structure in their lives to function well in the world, but they may struggle with this, especially when they are younger. If you provide structure, encourage communication, and enforce rules, then you will make it easier for your child to learn and become better in the future. This will also help children with ADHD do better at school because they will feel more relaxed in the classroom.

Children with ADHD need structure and routine in their lives to succeed at school and elsewhere. If they do not have this, they may struggle with the tasks they must learn to fit into society.

Parents can also create a routine for themselves so they know what they need to do each day. This will give them a sense of control over their lives. They can create routines around how things are done, which will help them handle daily tasks easier and feel better about themselves and their lives.

A routine can be as simple as setting up a specific time each day to exercise, such as going for a stroll or jogging outside. Having a routine for your child can be very beneficial because it helps them feel more confident and comfortable in their lives. It gives the child a sense of control over his or her feelings and emotions. The child will not have to worry about what is going to happen next, and he or she will be able to feel more secure about life overall.

Children with ADHD can benefit greatly from a structured life, as they often do not handle situations as well as their non-ADHD counterparts. Having structure in place can help them to keep their emotions together better at school and elsewhere. Without this, they can feel lost or unsure of themselves because they are unable to predict what will happen next. This can cause them to become worried and upset.

Routines you can practice at home with your family:

- Create a specific time each day to take care of chores.

- Make sure everyone in the family has set chores to do each day, and try to stick to the same chores for everyone.

- Establish a time each night when your child is expected to complete their homework. If you notice your child hasn't finished their homework, take away his/her evening activities until the work is completed (i.e., computer/tv/phone).

- Have a specific bedtime routine that can include reading, or drinking warm milk.

- Have designated times for meals and stick with it!

- Establish boundaries; if your child gets angry because you told them they couldn't do something, let them know the outcomes of their actions. (e.g., "You can't play video games all day like that because it will make you too tired to get your homework done.")

- Have family meetings throughout the week; communicate frequently; share complaints; help each other out!

- Have fun with life!

- Always have a calendar or planner on hand, so you don't forget appointments.

- Have an emergency kit in the car so your child can have a snack if they get stuck somewhere because of terrible weather, etc.

- Attend family meetings, meals, and activities together.

- Make sure all family members comprehend what is expected of them.

- Establish a routine when entertaining guests.

- Don't try to change your children's routines. Encourage consistency with the events you have planned.

- Be realistic when planning activities for your family;

don't expect your child to do things you would have trouble with! If your child gets overwhelmed, skip certain parts of what you are planning so they can handle it better.

- Talk to everyone in the house about anger management, tantrums, and other issues that affect everyone in the family, so there is no confusion or misunderstandings when it comes to confronting problems.

- Establish positive ways to deal with anger. If your child has a meltdown, let him/her take a break and calm down in his/her room.

- Establish positive ways to deal with frustration.

- Don't go overboard with discipline; use positive reinforcement to get your point across.

- Don't engage in power struggles; be firm, set boundaries and allow for your child to make decisions when they are appropriate.

- Establish routines for fun activities; having fun helps children learn better, work with others better, and feel better about life!

-

Practice good time management skills yourself; model them for your family members, and encourage them to do it independently!

A typical day would go as follows for a child with ADHD:

- Breakfast - There is a known routine for this meal that helps your child to feel more at ease and more excited for his day. Examples of routine include: setting the table, helping with clean up, talking about school events, etc.

- After breakfast - Set out his school materials. Demonstrate to your child how to put on his shoes and tie them tightly so he won't wiggle them off during the day.

- Have your child help put his or her backpack on.

- If possible, have your child move closer to you while he walks out the door. This is to help secure his attention and focus on you rather than on leaving home.

- After school, praise your child for coming home on time. Let them know that you are delighted with them.

- Encourage your child to bring in homework and assignments. Encourage creativity and imagination in children!

- When the daily chores are completed, most children will go straight for video games, TV, or playing on the computer without any thought of homework. This is where it becomes necessary to be proactive. Occasionally ask your child what they are doing during homework time, in order to check in.

- Dinner – There are different dining methods, but having a routine helps children feel more organized and organized children perform better.

- Bedtime – Once the chores are done for that day, the next step is to prepare for bedtime. This can be challenging for some kids because bedtime usually means an end to fun activities for the day. This is where having fun routines and routines to get ready for bed will help ease your child into a routine that helps them to relax and go to sleep.

Remember, routines are helpful for children with ADHD. If your child doesn't like the routine, try changing it up. After they adjust, continue with the new routine.

Strategies for solving problems

1. Praise and reward modeling

Many children with ADHD demonstrate a tendency to be noncompliant and disruptive. Fortunately, parents and caregivers can take steps to address this problem by incorporating praise and rewards into their home environment. Parents and caregivers can praise and reward compliant behavior in several ways. Firstly, when praising the child's effort it is helpful to be specific about what you are praising so that the child understands what he or she did right. Reward can also be incorporated into the child's routines. If your child with ADHD is having a rough time putting away his or her toys, you may want to switch to a different on-task approach for a week. This means you can praise or reward your child for putting away his or her toys, but only if the child does so without being asked. By doing so, you allow your child to demonstrate his or her ability to do what you are asking despite the fact that it was not expected. If the child is rewarded for a specific behavior, they are more likely to learn what behaviors are acceptable and be motivated to do it again.

2. Establish a daily schedule

Children with ADHD often display a great deal of impulsivity and can fail to complete a task if it is not interesting. To minimize these problems, parents and caregivers can establish a daily schedule to help their children focus on one activity at a time. This could mean establishing a time for homework, an activity for after school, and assigning chores for the rest of the evening.

3. Reduce television viewing

Parents should take steps to minimize the amount of television viewing over the course of the day, encouraging their children to engage in other activities.

4. Limit access to technology

Children with ADHD often have increased exposure to screen technologies, including computers, video games, and cell phones. They are also more likely to use technology excessively. As a result of excessive exposure to these technologies, children with ADHD are more likely to become increasingly bored and stressed out over time. This is because electronic media provide the same stimuli every day and do not provide a variety of new experiences.

5. Exercise

A child that suffers from ADHD sometimes lacks the ability to self-regulate their energy levels. Regular exercise can be beneficial, as studies have shown that aerobic exercise improves several aspects of brain function, including attention and inhibition control.

6. Reduce sugar intake

Research have shown that increased sugar intake is associated with increased hyperactivity in children. Because of this, parents and caregivers need to limit sugar intake as much as possible.

7. Increase calcium intake

Decreased calcium levels have also been associated with ADHD behavior. Calcium is important for maintaining certain neurotransmitters in the brain and helps to reduce muscle tension, which is common among children with ADHD.

8. Improve diet

A wide variety of studies have indicated that dietary factors such as carbohydrate consumption, fat consumption, and saturated fats consumption are all linked to an abnormal dopamine system, which could potentially lead to hyperactive behavior.

9. Avoid artificial food coloring and preservatives

Parents should avoid excessive use of artificial food coloring and preservatives that contain Bisphenol A (BPA) to minimize exposure to this substance.

Having Honest Conversations with Your Children About ADHD

Parents of children with ADHD may feel guilty about what their child is going through and may even wonder if they are responsible for their child's disorder. Moving past this guilt takes a lot of work and time. When parents set good examples at home, the child will feel more motivated to work harder at school. Parents of children with ADHD need to understand that they are not responsible for their child's disorder, and they need to let go of their feelings of guilt so they can motivate their children more effectively. Their child's behavior can improve over time, especially if the proper treatment strategies and positive reinforcement encourage a child to work harder and do better in school or at home.

Another thing that parents of children with ADHD need to do is explain the effect their child's behavior has on other family members. This can be very challenging because many parents feel embarrassed by their child's behavior, especially if they are having trouble at school. Parents of children with ADHD need to explain to other family members what they are experiencing so that there can be support within the home. Asking for help from others is essential, and it allows the child to feel more comfortable within the home.

The final thing parents of children with ADHD need to do is give their child positive attention. This may seem like an obvious point, but it is vital for children with ADHD that positive attention is given at all times. When children with ADHD take medication, they may feel sad or angry that someone else is controlling their behavior. The loss of control can make the child feel as if their parents no longer love them. Parents need to make sure they give positive attention to their children at all times, even when the child's behavior is bad.

Parenting a child with ADHD takes a lot of work. Parents need to play different roles that require them to be more involved in the life of their children. It is also important for parents to learn from other parents who have been in similar positions and listen to their advice and support from professionals who understand the disorder. Children with ADHD need discipline, but they also need understanding and encouragement in order to work harder.

CHAPTER 6: PARENTS AND ADHD

P arents with ADHD have particular challenges, including coping with their symptoms, managing the demands of work and family, and managing their child's behavior. Parents with ADHD have the same stresses as other parents but also have issues that are unique to having ADHD themselves. However, it is important to note that, except for the cost and inconvenience of extra services and medications, having a child with ADHD does not appear to affect parents' marital satisfaction or parental stress more than it does that of parents whose children do not have ADHD.

Parents with ADHD have deficits in cognitive skills and thus may encounter particular difficulty in parenting their children. Research suggests that mothers and fathers with ADHD show deficits in the global problem-solving skills required for effective parenting as a whole. In particular, mothers with ADHD have been found to have significantly lower levels of self-regulation, and lower levels of planning and organization than mothers without ADHD. Fathers with ADHD, despite performing better on some of the cognitive tasks than fathers without ADHD, show significant deficits in executive control abilities.

Parents with ADHD can be overwhelmed by their symptoms and may not recognize the same symptoms in their children. As with other behavioral problems, parental perceptions of ADHD themselves are more important than parenting methods for regulating the child's behavior. Parents with ADHD have difficulty detecting and assessing symptoms, particularly when aggravated or masked by another factor.

The more severe the parent's symptoms are, the greater difficulty they have in modifying that behavior. Parents with ADHD report more behavior problems in their children than parents without ADHD do. These parents attribute those problem behaviors disproportionately to external circumstances and show less skill in using appropriate strategies for modifying that behavior than those without ADHD. Parents with ADHD have more difficulty "putting themselves in their child's shoes" than non-ADHD parents. However, parenting strategies that appear to be effective for parents with ADHD are the same as those reported to be effective for parents without ADHD.

This chapter aims to raise awareness concerning the challenges of parenting with ADHD and highlight suggestions for increasing their confidence in dealing with these challenges. *Raising an Explosive Child* can help parents who have experienced or currently experience the challenges of raising an ADHD child by providing solutions. Parents will learn how they can become more confident in themselves; it is not about "perfection" but about "acceptance," and with acceptance comes confidence.

The Challenges of Parenting with ADHD

A full understanding of challenges experienced by parents with ADHD is crucial to obtaining the support one needs from peers and professionals. Parents with ADHD often do not fully understand their own experiences until they undergo individual psychotherapy or couples counseling.

As with all situations that involve raising a child, there are unique challenges to parenting with ADHD. The relationship between both parents has to be positive for it to work well. The attitude of the other parent has to be open and supportive toward the parent who has ADHD. If the parents are not comfortable cooperatively working together, there can be serious consequences for both parents and their children.

There are often problems with the early attachment relationship between the ADHD parent and their child. The child may be difficult to read or may not show signs of having a close relationship with either parent. Mothers with ADHD tend to have more difficulties in their attachments with their children than fathers, as they tend to have more difficulty regulating emotions. In addition, social skills deficits tend to increase the difficulties of parenting. No studies prove that non-ADHD parents have a poorer relationship with their children than those without ADHD. However, a study indicates that parents with ADHD have more difficulties in their early attachment formation than those without ADHD. As the parents' relationship with both each other and the child is of utmost importance, it is recommended that they receive counseling in parenting skills. Some skills need to be taught and practiced in order for all to succeed.

The emotional state of the ADHD parent can be an important issue when raising children. The more distressed the parent, the less able they will be to effectively respond to their child's needs. It is more difficult for these parents to regulate their emotions than others, so emotions tend to cycle from high to lows much faster than those without ADHD. In addition, these parents tend to have lower self-esteem and greater levels of depression compared with those without ADHD. These factors can lead to feelings of discouragement, hopelessness, and anger. Low self-esteem makes it more difficult for the ADHD parent to be open with or supportive of other family members. Low self-esteem is associated with less effective parental behavior in parenting tasks. Low self-esteem can interfere with helping the child learn to self-regulate. Depressed mothers have been shown to have poorer relationships with their children than other mothers. The family structure may also be affected by the emotions experienced by the ADHD parents. The stress caused by ADHD symptoms may cause conflict within the family, which can lead to family dysfunction, including marital conflict and divorce, physical abuse, child abuse, and neglect.

Although there is no specific test of the parenting skills of an ADHD parent, one may develop over time through learning and practice. These parenting skills can be used to detect their strengths and weaknesses when confronted with a child with ADHD. For example, parents will often have a negative perception of their abilities in disciplining their children when, in reality, they are not as bad as they think they are. In order for parents to become more aware of these weaknesses, it is recommended that they practice positively reinforcing behaviors in front of a mirror or video themselves while responding to their children. This will enable them to become more practiced in utilizing these skills.

The Importance of Getting a Diagnosis of ADHD in a Parent

When a child is diagnosed with ADHD, the parents should schedule an appointment with a mental health professional for themselves as well as their child. The mental health professional will assess a parent for psychological issues and/or their capacity to handle a child with ADHD. Parents with ADHD have been known to have low self-esteem and question their ability to raise their child properly. They also have their own emotional or behavioral disorders that affect parenting behaviors.

It is common for the parent with ADHD to experience anger, frustration, and resentment because of their child's behavior. These emotions can generate an intense emotional response that may be directed at the child. The parent may not realize that this feeling of anger is due to how poorly they are able to problem-solve, thanks to their disorder. The parent with ADHD may feel incompetent and depressed, which may influence their interactions with their child. The parent may also act impulsively or more aggressively than they would with another child.

It is crucial for parents to know how their ADHD affects their parenting of an ADHD child. This can be gained through proper education of the causes and effects that ADHD has on the family, effective use of positive parenting skills, and therapy to help them manage their issues in a non-judgmental way. In addition, the parent needs to have strong support from other family members, including grandparents, and there should be a close relationship with at least one other adult in the home.

Adapting to the child's ADHD (or other) disorder is an adjustment that parents must make. With good parenting skills, however, it can be easier for parents to adapt to their child's behavior, promoting the child's overall health and well-being. Once teachers and other adults learn how to work with children with ADHD and demonstrate a strong belief in the child and family, it will help both the teacher and the family. Teachers often bring up issues of ADHD children when they come to parent group meetings. They may provide specific suggestions about how parents can best respond to their children with ADHD at home or school.

Parent-Child Interactions

The following are some of the difficulties parents with ADHD may have when dealing with their children. These are areas where parents can use the most assistance.

Having difficulty in setting limits for their children.

This includes problems in establishing rules, managing inappropriate behavior, meting out discipline, and using ineffective but common responses to problem behaviors (e.g., physical force, verbal threats). Commonly used responses to problem behaviors include physical punishment, verbal threats, ridicule, harsh criticism, or expressing great annoyance. The parent may be unable to clearly communicate rules or expectations due to not being able to organize thoughts well enough to convey a clear message of what needs to be done.

Many parents with ADHD utilize a "do as I say, not as I do" approach.

This behavior is characterized by the parent's endorsement of a certain behavioral expectation being followed, but the parent refuses to personally follow these same expectations. A common example is a parent who prohibits his/her child from watching television on school nights, but then the parent turns on the television after that child has gone to bed. In some cases, this type of response from a parent may be used because they expect their child to have higher standards than adults have for themselves.

Being inconsistent in the discipline procedures used with their children.

This type of response is particularly problematic for an ADHD child who comes to expect that they can get away with unacceptable behaviors without consequence. It is common for the parent to blame the child's poor performance on his/her "slow" mental processing. For example, a parent might excuse inappropriate behavior because the child was distracted or didn't hear what was said or was talking with someone else at the time. The parent may also be easily distracted by other feedback or stimuli in the environment, which leads them to have difficulty staying on task.

Parents with ADHD may be inattentive and may not respond to their child's requests in a timely manner.

This inattention is due to the parent being preoccupied with other tasks that they find more interesting or even doing something that may be inappropriate. To recover from this behavior, the parent will usually rush through the given task and attempt to make amends for this bad behavior.

They may have difficulty controlling anger when addressing misbehavior problems in their child.

Parental anger is common when dealing with an ADHD child; however, ADHD in the parent can affect how they discipline their child or communicate expectations. The parent often makes excuses for their child's inappropriate behavior or ignores it altogether. The parent may experience anger toward other family members or other people in the environment, but this anger is directed towards the child because of his/her negative behaviors.

Parents with ADHD may find themselves repeating instructions to their child which they should already know.

They might repeat themselves three or four times without getting the expected response from their child. The parents will take this as an indication that their child is either "lazy" or "trying to get out of doing what they are told."

Parenting Effectively with ADHD

Working with a therapist will provide an environment in which you can feel comfortable and safe enough to work through your issues. A therapist can provide you with information and ideas on how to help your child succeed in school and in life. Many parents find it beneficial to seek therapy when their child or children are between the ages of 10–18 years old when the effects of ADHD are reaching their highest point. It is common for ADHD children in this age range to experience self-esteem, academic and social issues. The therapy will focus on helping the individual learn coping skills that will assist them in dealing with hard situations that may arise at home or in school. The therapist will work with the individual to determine whether they have ADHD or a related disorder and then help them discover what areas of their lives are affected the most by their disorder.

Here are some strategies for parenting with ADHD:

Give yourself permission to make mistakes.

It is hard enough to parent someone who has ADHD, without also having the disorder yourself! But please don't forget that it is all about the "us," not the "them." If you are struggling or feeling overwhelmed, give yourself permission to pull back for a few days or weeks. This will also allow you to find other strategies that may work for your family. Give your child alone time daily. When the child is younger, this should be no more than 20 minutes daily, but as they grow older, this will increase.

Exposure to bright lights can help.

Parents can use brighter and more colorful lighting during the day and use the dimmer at night. If possible, turn off or block out excess light from other sources. Some children may also benefit from the use of a sleep light for bedtime.

Medications

Medicines used to treat ADHD in children can be divided into stimulants and non-stimulants. Prior to the 1980s, the only drug available for treating ADHD in children was a stimulant called Ritalin. In the 1980s, Adderall came out, followed by other stimulants such as Dexedrine and Cylert. In 1996, Strattera came on the market as a non-stimulant to treat ADHD symptoms in children and adults.

In the 2000s, Concerta and Metadate ER were introduced as extended-release forms of methylphenidate. Atomoxetine

(Strattera) was approved for the treatment of symptoms of ADHD in adults and children over age 6 in 2006.

The non-stimulant medication guanfacine (Intuniv) was approved for the treatment of symptoms of ADHD in children on December 29, 2007. Medically safe doses of guanfacine are approved for adults and children over six years old only.

An extended-release formulation of Aptensio, Targiniq, Targinq ER, and Armodafinil was approved by the FDA in February 2016. This is a non-stimulant medication used to treat the symptoms associated with ADHD in adults and children over six years old.

The effectiveness of ADHD drugs has been shown to be significantly lower than was initially claimed by the pharmaceutical companies. In particular, a Princeton University study found that 89% of privately insured children who had been prescribed medication for ADHD received doses that were either too high or not high enough. "Psychostimulant medications have been advocated as first-line treatments for ADHD; however, we found that most children prescribed these medications do not meet treatment guidelines, and many are on dosages above recommended levels."

ADHD is usually treated with a blend of regular and special education and psychological (psychiatric) services and/or medications (i.e., stimulant or non-stimulant) to reduce symptoms. Treatment can be long-term or lifelong, but some aspects of the condition may improve with age.

Stimulants

Stimulant medications should be used as needed. It is important that the medication be used in conjunction with behavioral counseling and other treatments such as working with a therapist. The goal should be to avoid taking stimulants unless the child cannot function without them. ADHD stimulant medications increase activity in the ADHD brain while reducing activity in the non-ADHD brain regions, so they help improve attention and concentration, but they can also cause hyperactivity and other behavior problems if not followed by suitable behavioral reinforcement strategies and other treatments such as therapy and learning strategies for self-management of ADHD behaviors.

Stimulants keep the child up and effectively focus them so they can take in information. They also improve problem solving, which is an issue commonly associated with ADHD. It has been shown that methylphenidate can cause aggression if taken before bedtime, so it should not be taken after 8 pm. These medications should only be used over short periods of time because of the risks associated with prolonged use. They also should not be used to manage severe ADHD due to possible risks of tics and aggressive behavior. Stimulants can cause mood swings and can be very addictive and dangerous to the growth of a child.

Non-stimulants

Non-stimulant medications may also be taken, but stimulants are more effective. Non-stimulants include clonidine, which is used to treat high blood pressure, as well as atomoxetine, which is not currently FDA approved for ADHD but has been shown to be effective in clinical trials. They may be prescribed as well if the stimulant medications are not helping or cannot be used for various reasons. These medications must be monitored closely due to their potential for abuse and other side effects. They can also cause depression and mood swings as well as sleep problems.

Behavioral Interventions

Behavioral therapy

This has been presented in clinical trials to be the most effective therapy approach in treating ADHD. Behavior therapy focuses on teaching developing skills in the areas of the organization, prioritizing tasks, time management, completing assignments, managing anxiety or anger when confronted with a behavioral expectation that is hard to complete, and dealing with specific situations when they arise. The therapist will work with the parent to understand their specific areas of weakness when dealing with their ADHD child's behavior problems, and then help them identify an appropriate behavioral response that will teach their child how to improve their behavior in that specific situation. They will then record this strategy and use it with their child until the selected behavior changes.

Behavior management classes are a more structured approach to improving social skills. The programs cover topics such as assertiveness, anger control, stress management, communication skills and self-esteem. Parents learn how to manage stress by learning how to take better care of themselves and use more positive ways to deal with the frustrations that arise when dealing with an ADHD child. A lot of children with Attention Deficit Hyperactivity Disorder have low self-esteem because they are not achieving academically or socially like their peers, and their ADHD is frequently blamed for their problems.

Cognitive-behavioral Therapy (CBT)

CBT is a form of psychotherapy that centers on the areas of judgment, beliefs, learning, and thought patterns. It has been shown to be effective for ADHD. CBT can help parents stop automatic negative thinking about ADHD and learn new ways of thinking that will transform their approach to challenging situations with their child.

Cognitive-behavioral therapy can be used to treat a wide variety of negative thoughts, feelings, and behaviors that may result from ADHD. In the area of ADHD behavior, this therapy works by showing parents how to overcome the tendency to blame themselves for their child's misbehavior and learn new behavior management strategies that will eliminate these problems. They will learn to notice when their child misbehaves and to make a plan for completing necessary tasks before the misbehavior occurs. It is important to note that children with ADHD often try to get others to take the blame when they misbehave. Cognitive-behavioral therapy can be good in helping parents react to their child's misbehavior in a calm, non-punitive manner; and yet still teach the child that this type of behavior is unacceptable.

CBT works best when it is concentrated on the areas where the parent is experiencing the most problems. Parents who are having problems making decisions or knowing how to make good choices for their family will be helped by exposure therapy (i.e., exposure to specific situations that may arise) to help them become less nervous and more confident in their decision-making ability. The other two areas of focus for CBT are social skills training (social problem-solving) and behavioral rehearsal (to learn how to behave appropriately in specific situations that arise).

Under the supervision of a qualified therapist, problem-solving skills can be taught to better manage daily hassles. This approach to therapy helps the ADHD child improve the ability to think through problems and feel more comfortable about completing tasks. For example, giving instructions for homework or other tasks or giving tips on how to complete a task will make this a simpler process for the parent. It will also make it easier for the child to prioritize tasks and see more clearly how to organize their time.

Social skills training (SST)

SST is based on the idea that many children with ADHD have difficulty with social interactions. The goal of SST is to teach the child how to respond appropriately in various situations, such as sharing or not interrupting. Parents are trained on how to help their children learn how to act around other children, be assertive without anger, and make friends more easily. It focuses on teaching the parents how they can help their child manage negative feelings that may arise during social interactions, such as feeling left out or being unable to do what others do. The parent will learn ways to help their child handle these feelings in a positive manner so they can continue engaging in the conversation or activity with fewer problems.

Parent-child interaction therapy (PCIT)

This is a form of psychotherapy that specifically targets the relationship between parent and child. Parents are taught how to improve their relationship with their child by learning positive ways to respond when their child misbehaves. It teaches parents how to discourage negative behavior in a supportive, non-threatening manner that does not lead to feelings of shame or failure in the child.

PCIT focuses on the interaction between parent and child, rather than focusing on the child's behavior problems alone. The therapist will help parents learn how to give feedback in a way that encourages good behavior. Parents are taught specific skills (i.e., problem-solving, observation, and critical thinking) that they can use to solve social or behavioral problems that may arise with their children.

PCIT is based on the idea that parents model good behavior for their children. If a parent misbehaves, a child will usually also be negatively affected. Teaching positive ways of handling emotions and bad behavior can help parents and children more effectively interact with one another.

Behavioral rehearsal (BR)

This is a technique that helps children learn to behave in non-disruptive ways by helping them imagine how they would feel if they were unable to complete a task. They are taught how to anticipate the consequences of their actions and then try not to experience these consequences. Parents are taught how to aid their children to practice behavior changes that will help them become more successful. For example, teaching the child what is likely to happen if he or she has a tantrum will help them decrease the likelihood of being thrown out of class or being excluded from activities, games, or social groups. Parents are taught to avoid negative physical punishment and other techniques that traumatize the child.

Behavioral rehearsal can also be used by parents to help children understand how to behave appropriately in shopping situations. The child is taught to imagine how they would feel if they want an item that is not available. This method can help the child relax into the situation, visualize how it will go, and then try not to experience these feelings. Once the child is able to manage the emotional response, this method can be used for other similar experiences.

When using behavioral rehearsal, it is important that the child is able to practice using the new behavior in a safe environment. Parents who are seeking treatment for their children should seek the assistance of a qualified therapist when undertaking behavioral rehearsal.

Consultations for this approach will meet with both parents and therapists to create an appropriate plan for re-training the child in specific situations. The goal of behavioral rehearsal is not to change how they feel but how they behave in different situations so they can be successful without experiencing stress or distress. Using behavioral rehearsal with children who have specific phobias will require additional training from a therapist before the method can be used by parents on their own.

Self-talk rehearsal (STR)

STR focuses on helping a child learn positive behaviors through behavior rehearsal exercises that are specific to their situation or event, such as a doctor's visit or a parent-teacher conference. This approach helps a child learn to experience a non-stressful outcome in stressful situations.

STR can help a child prepare for difficult tasks or events. Self-talk involves understanding the challenge, anticipating the outcome, visualizing how one will feel if they manage the challenge, and then actually experiencing these feelings by completing the task or event.

This method is most effective when parents set aside time daily for their children to complete self-talk rehearsal exercises. This will help them develop positive skills that can be used in their daily lives and become more confident and successful over time. When setting up self-talk exercises, it is important that the child understands that this approach will not allow them to avoid their challenges, but rather help prepare them for what they will experience. It is important that the parent not "talk over" the child's negative self-talk and help them change it to positive self-talk.

The PTG (Parent-Taught-Group)

This is a form of behavior therapy that helps parents teach their children skills that will help them become more successful. Parents are taught how to use group strategies to encourage positive behaviors in their children by providing positive feedback and identifying bad behavior with strategies that do not traumatize the child. Parents are given the tools they need, and instructed on how best to use them in different situations with their children. The sessions are designed so that parents can easily understand the principles of behavior therapy, learn new skills, provide positive feedback, set limits on inappropriate behaviors, and troubleshoot problems as they arise.

The PTG model is designed to be as flexible as possible so it can be used with children of all ages and is not limited to those living in high-risk environments. The goal of PTG skill-building sessions is to help parents teach their children how to behave appropriately in their everyday lives.

Positive Parenting

It has been said that positive parenting fosters optimal child development.

The term "positive parenting" has been used by many researchers and practitioners to describe a generalized strategy of encouraging appropriate and adaptive behavior and emotions in children, as opposed to "negative" parenting strategies that encourage disruptive or problematic behaviors. Positive parenting methods have been reported to be associated with a wide range of positive outcomes for children, including increased cognitive abilities, greater family cohesion and stability, and less aggression in children. Conversely, negative parenting has been associated with several negative outcomes for children such as stress and anxiety, greater aggression in the child, poorer intellectual development, and an increased likelihood that the child will exhibit antisocial behaviors in adulthood.

The science of positive parenting is rapidly expanding. Hundreds of research studies in the last two decades have shown that positive parenting strategies are associated with positive outcomes for children. The results of these studies show that many different types of positive parenting strategies are beneficial, and each approach (e.g., sensitivity, social support, or reinforcement) has unique benefits for children. Parents who use one or more types of positive parenting strategies appear to be better at facilitating communications in their families; in addition, they are less likely to report stress in their family life than parents who do not use all three types of positive parenting strategies (i.e., sensitive, inclusive, and responsive parents).

Habit Reversal Training (HRT)

This is an approach that helps children become more successful at completing tasks by teaching them how to think about their behavior as it relates to the task, rather than as a way to escape from the situation. HRT focuses on teaching a child how to replace their automatic behaviors with purposeful ones, which will minimize acting out and increase self-control. It is based on the assumption that if a child first thinks about what they will do instead of how they will feel, they are less likely to engage in problematic behavior.

HRT helps the child practice changes in their behavior. The child is taught to interrupt a task or activity that is not working and then imagine or rehearse a new behavior that works well. This will help them regulate their emotions and successfully engage in a different task, which can be difficult for children with learning disabilities to do on their own. HRT is ideal for use with children who have autism spectrum disorders, as well as those who have difficulty learning attention management skills, problem-solving skills, and self-control. The technique can also be used by parents of children with other diagnosed conditions such as Oppositional Defiant Disorder (ODD), anxiety disorders, or learning disorders.

HRT is a way to replace bad habits with new ones. An example of this would be if a child has a temper tantrum when he is unable to complete his homework assignment on time and then isolates himself in his room and refuses to talk to his parents about his homework problems. If an HRT approach was implemented, the therapist would help him learn how to first interrupt his behavior and then imagine doing something else that would work better instead. The therapist would also teach the parent how to intervene when they see their child beginning to feel overwhelmed with their outbursts and need a break from the situation.

In order to determine the most effective treatment for a child's ADHD, psychologists must rely on a three-pronged approach: a diagnostic evaluation, a battery of behavioral tests, and observations of the child. Cognitive testing is generally not necessary unless the child is suspected of having learning difficulties or psychosocial problems that might be related to attention. In many cases, determination of the cause(s) of the behaviors can be accomplished through interviews with friends and parents as well as classroom teachers and school reports.

The biggest challenge for most parents of children with ADHD is finding ways to help their children. This can be very difficult because they are most likely exhausted from taking care of the child themselves.

Teachers and other adults should recognize that parents with ADHD may not be able to understand what their children experience or how they learn. Parents of children with ADHD must learn strategies for promoting effective learning and behavior in order to get their child's attention and get him to listen to them.

Parents of children with ADHD may feel overwhelmed by the responsibilities of taking care of a child and may struggle with letting down their defenses and expressing their concerns and frustrations about parenting an ADHD child.

There is significant variability in how parents of children with ADHD deal with disciplinary issues. Some resort to the use of physical punishment, while others try to reason with their child. Some parents attempt to control their anger and frustration by ignoring misbehaviors, while others repeat themselves over and over again when disciplining their children.

There is no singular correct approach when disciplining a child with ADHD. Depending on the severity of the misconduct, parents can choose different strategies. If a child is very proactive in misbehaving, the entire household will have to be involved in implementing various strategies. If discipline is needed, parents will have to select the "best" method.

PART 3 - ADHD AT SCHOOL

CHAPTER 7: IDENTIFYING ADHD IN EDUCATIONAL SETTINGS

Often, the symptoms of ADHD remain undetected until a child is at school, which can impede the child's success. It is often hard for teachers and others to recognize ADHD in children, and they may react adversely to it; this can be especially true if the child exhibits negative behavioral traits such as defiance and anger. Parents and teachers must be vigilant to recognize ADHD at school. Awareness is the first step towards prevention and treatment.

Some signs of ADHD with a child in school include:

• Excessive Daydreaming

When a child daydreams excessively in class, it can suggest that they are losing interest in what is happening in class and becoming bored with what they are learning. The teacher may (incorrectly) perceive the child as not paying attention or being disruptive when, in fact, the child's mind is wandering. The teacher should be aware that children with ADHD often spend more time daydreaming than their peers and distinguish between daydreaming and inattentive behavior.

• Excessive Talking

When the child is talking excessively in class, especially if they are addressing more than four people, it can suggest that the child has excessive chatter and is easily bored. The teacher may (incorrectly) perceive the child as being noisy or disrupting when, in fact, the child may be less self-aware of their tongue than their peers are. The teacher should be aware that children with ADHD are often talkative, possibly because they miss in-depth conversations at home.

• Disruption to Classwork

The student's behavior in class can often indicate whether or not there is a problem with attention or hyperactivity. If the child is constantly moving, distracting others, or otherwise disrupting their environment, this can suggest ADHD. The teacher should be aware that children with ADHD often need to move around and may not sit still for long periods of time, so it is essential to recognize that this behavior may result from an underlying condition rather than just a behavioral trait.

• Lack of Concentration

Often the inappropriate behavior of the child is misinterpreted by teachers and peers as a lack of concentration. When teachers and classmates see a child fidgeting and displaying unusual behavior such as jumping up from their seat during class, they may attribute the behavior to lack of attention rather than ADHD. Unfortunately, this can be harmful to the child, as they are being labeled as being disruptive. When the teacher suspects ADHD is the underlying issue, they must prepare themselves to be supportive and reassuring to the child rather than punitive.

• Failure to Complete Homework

A lack of motivation may indicate ADHD. A child will often be given homework or asked to complete activities in class, but if these are not done at home, it suggests that the child may not be able to stay on task or have an inability to self-motivate. Teachers must inquire about why homework isn't done or if there is some other reason for incompletion (such as forgetfulness) in order to correctly diagnose ADHD.

• Regression

Some children may regress when they are in class, indicating an underlying problem with ADHD. Often when a child is given homework or asked to complete activities in class, they are excited about learning or completing the tasks. Still, when they are doing these tasks at home, they may not see the value behind them and may not be inspired to complete them. Conversely, teachers must be aware that children with ADHD often have problems staying on task at school but find it easier to focus at home.

• Impatience

Children with ADHD often have trouble waiting their turn or being patient. They may interrupt other children or become impatient when waiting for the teacher to respond to their requests. Teachers must be aware that children with ADHD can find it hard to wait in lines, wait while others are talking or wait for instructions, and act out when they cannot fulfill these requests.

• Restlessness

Restless children can often be distracted easily and lose focus on what is happening in class. The teacher must be aware that the child may not understand why they are asked to stay focused when their minds are easily distracted by other things, such as ticking clocks or blinking lights. Teachers should be prepared for this, as it is common in children with ADHD.

• Disorganization

Children who are disorganized can often be seen as lazy or lackadaisical. They may be unaware that the classroom is meant to have a certain structure and may become frustrated when they don't understand how it works. Teachers must be aware of this problem and approach the situation by explaining the classroom structure, being patient while answering questions about procedures, being available to answer questions, and being vigilant to recognize the symptoms of ADHD.

• Moodiness

Children who are moody are often easily distracted by loud noises or harsh lighting in class. Teachers should anticipate the child's reaction and approach it with patience.

• Loss of Interest

Children who lose interest in learning may lose focus on what is happening in class. When a child has lost interest, they may appear distracted, daydream, or even fall asleep during class.

Often children with ADHD are emotionally detached from their teachers, and the teacher may believe the child doesn't care. Teachers must be aware that children with ADHD may act indifferently because of their inability to focus on what is happening in the class. When the teacher realizes this, they can approach the situation with patience and understanding.

Recognizing ADHD as a Learning Disorder

Children with ADHD are not stupid, nor are they bad children. They are children who have difficulty concentrating long enough to do what needs to be done. This is purely due to their ADHD.

ADHD does not mean that children will never learn anything; it only means that the process of learning may be more difficult for them. Children with ADHD can learn things just as well as other children, but they may require more time, effort, and patience to master the same skills or tasks.

Children with ADHD do not need to be treated with resentment or frustration. They are simply individuals who learn in ways that are different from others. For this reason, they may need special attention and care that is catered specifically towards their learning style.

The first step to helping children that suffer from ADHD is to recognize that there is a problem. This is a very hard step for many teachers, parents, and caretakers, as many believe the child is simply being disobedient or lazy. However, when one learns to recognize the symptoms of ADHD in others, it allows them to provide the help required before any permanent damage is done. ADHD symptoms in children can be recognized through watching their behavior. It is usually much more obvious in young children; many things that are dismissed as bad behavior in older children or adults would not be tolerated for very long in young children.

As ADHD is a learning disorder, it is possible that some children will not be diagnosed until they reach school age. It does not mean they do not have ADHD; it only means that parents or caretakers never noticed the symptoms. This is common, and many people are diagnosed with ADHD after they reach school age, or even later.

As a means of helping children with ADHD learn, teachers often have to teach them in a new way. This can be frustrating for many teachers and parents, but it can be made easier when the teacher understands the learning process of children with ADHD.

CHAPTER 8: TEACHING STRATEGIES FOR CHILDREN WITH ADHD

Teachers spend a great amount of time educating children, and thus they must have a great deal of patience. When teaching children with ADHD, teachers need to be aware that the disorder may cause children to be unfocused, forgetful, and inattentive. Teachers should ensure that their expectations are reasonable.

Children with ADHD need to be taught certain skills that will make their lives easier. These skills may be in the areas of the organization, time management, communication, and social interaction. Children with ADHD generally need frequent reminders to assist them in completing tasks.

Teachers need to understand what causes distractions for children with ADHD. They must adapt their teaching style so it will be most effective for these children. Teachers should structure their lessons so that they are short, concise, and straightforward. They should try not to use too many words or examples, as it will be difficult for the children with ADHD to keep track of them all.

There are many different methods that teachers can use to help children with ADHD. These techniques include giving children hints, showing evidence of progress, making mistakes the same way the child does, and setting problem-solving tasks.

Children with ADHD may become frustrated when they are given too much responsibility. Teachers should make it clear to these children that they can ask for help when necessary.

Children with ADHD are generally very social, but they may find it difficult to interact with others. However, there are some techniques that teachers can use to help children with ADHD interact better. They can help these children improve their listening skills by encouraging questions, allowing them to answer questions, and modeling how to be a good listener. Children with ADHD may become frustrated if they feel that no one understands them. Teachers should make sure that they spend time one-on-one with these children.

Children with ADHD may have difficulty concentrating for long periods, but they can continue learning and growing in new areas. In some cases, children with ADHD may benefit from having an individual plan designed specifically for their learning styles and abilities. This can help children with ADHD to focus more effectively on specific tasks while also focusing their minds on helpful information. This is an important step in developing the child with ADHD.

Children with ADHD are often very picky about what they will do in class. Thus, they choose subjects which they think will be exciting and enjoyable. It can be challenging for teachers and educators to recognize that these children's learning styles are different from others and that their minds simply want to focus on certain subjects.

Teachers can also help children with ADHD find ways to get over their differences and become more successful in the classroom by taking cues from them and allowing them to be creative and to work on their own. They can do this by involving the child in special projects that use their unique skills, such as art or music, or by providing one-on-one instruction.

Children with ADHD must be encouraged to make mistakes. This is something that educators need to understand, as it helps children with ADHD develop a greater sense of confidence while improving their self-esteem. It also teaches them that they are allowed to make mistakes while growing and learning new things.

As a teacher, you should not expect children with ADHD to be perfect or perform in a certain way. Allow them the freedom to try different activities and find their style of learning.

A teacher can help keep children's minds focused by being supportive. Children with ADHD may need different kinds of encouragement to learn. They will also need special attention throughout their schooling, especially when the work gets more difficult.

There are many things that a teacher or educator can do to develop a more positive learning environment for a child with ADHD. For example, teachers should be aware of the unique needs of children with ADHD and work on ways to help them achieve success in the classroom by putting together an individualized plan.

Interdisciplinary Team Meetings

At the time of diagnosis, parents need to determine what they will be expected to do to help their child with ADHD. Teachers often struggle with counseling children with ADHD, especially when one teacher has a different method from another. In many cases, parents are able to participate in a team meeting at the school involving all staff members responsible for the child. This may include the school psychologist, social worker, special education teacher, regular education teacher(s), and school counselor.

The purpose of the team meeting is to come up with an individualized educational plan (IEP) that will meet the child's needs in general education. The IEP may also include goals or benchmarks for academic performance and specific accommodations to help the child in their educational program. The team will also address the parents' concerns and expectations concerning their child's education. They will need to know what their child can learn and how they can help them at home.

Teachers can create a structured environment by setting rules necessary for learning to occur. For example, they may introduce the rule, "Raise your hand if you have a question."

When students have a disorder, teachers must work with them regularly so they can learn the material being taught in a classroom setting. By taking time to hear what the child with ADHD is saying and doing, teachers can create a more enthusiastic learning atmosphere. Teachers can also help children with ADHD by asking them to think about their goals. This way, they can discuss ideas and brainstorm about things they wish to achieve in future.

School Discipline

All school children are expected to follow school rules and regulations. This is especially true in the classroom. If a child has ADHD, they may not follow the rules or behave as others expect them to while in class. This can frustrate many teachers and educators. It can also frustrate other students because they may not understand why a child is not following the rules.

This is why some schools have adopted different programs to help control the discipline of students with problems. This can include 'time-out' rooms, where children can listen to music or read alone for a certain amount of time. It may also include 'cooling off' rooms, where the child has the chance to calm down.

Children with ADHD may need to see professionals, such as counselors and therapists, to deal with anxiety and stress in school. When children are stressed, they do not perform as well on assignments and tests. It is important to allow children with ADHD the opportunity to share their feelings with teachers or other professionals. This can lead to a more positive relationship between the child and teacher, which will help them study more effectively over the years.

It may take time for teachers to develop effective ways to deal with children with ADHD. Teachers may fear that singling the child out may hurt or upset the student, but understanding what they are going through will help everyone understand each other better.

There are two types of discipline in the classroom:

Minor discipline

The teacher usually does this to reward good behavior or to prohibit bad behavior. For example, if everyone is having fun in the classroom, but the child with ADHD keeps interrupting, the teacher may use time out to allow time for them to settle down. If they break the rules again after being given a warning, they will have a consequence. This can include a behavior chart where each student has a different bead color on a string, representing how many times they broke a rule during a given period.

The consequences that teachers give out should be specific and short. It is also important to not overuse them because the child may become used to punishment and no longer want to listen or cooperate.

One study that examined the effectiveness of four different classroom management approaches in elementary school children with ADHD was published in the *Journal of Applied Behavior Analysis*. The results showed that working to gain compliance by using positive incentives is more effective than reinforcing appropriate behaviors, ignoring, or negative punishment. Children who had more severe behavior problems or higher levels of inattention benefited most from rewards for correct answers on academic tasks. Poor-performing students with a low level of inattention did not respond to negative reinforcement.

In addition to positive incentives, giving children with ADHD specific directions may help them follow through because it helps them organize their work. Teachers must explain the assignment because children with ADHD may have trouble comprehending or remembering what they are supposed to do.

Teachers need to determine if a child has poor organization skills because of ADHD or is disorganized for other reasons. If it is a temporary problem, teachers can try to organize their materials more easily so the child can understand what needs to be accomplished in a given period.

Major discipline

If a child is acting out in a behavior that causes danger to themselves or others, they may be asked to exit the classroom. However, the school needs to have some way of dealing with these situations. They may call the child's parents and let them know what happened and what kind of punishment the child may face due to their actions. An ADHD child must still face consequences like any other student, but guidelines need to be established for parents and teachers beforehand. Providing a student with ADHD with support and coaching services may also help reduce disruptive behavior.

Teachers may have trouble managing classrooms if every student is given rewards or punishments because this makes it even harder for children to understand that the key aim is progress. Instead, teachers can use behaviors like "seat work" or "time-in."

At the start of the school year, teachers must establish rules and expectations so that students know what their responsibilities are. If the student with ADHD is being taught something particularly difficult, they must have more opportunities to learn it so that they don't have lower grades overall.

Developing a Classroom Management Plan

A classroom management plan should focus on issues related to organization. For example, teachers can use the plan to help students keep their backpacks organized. The teacher can also put together a system for organizing the students' desks. This may include the use of storage drawers or baskets under the desk to keep papers organized. Teachers can also help students create folders for each subject. Students should be encouraged to place their completed materials inside the folder so that it will be easy for them to access later.

The teacher can put reminders on the display board about upcoming test dates, holidays, and class trips. Other essential events that will take place during the year should also be posted so that students know what is expected of them at all times during school activities.

The classroom should be organized so that the students can easily see what is going on in each class. This can help them understand what assignments are due and when they must be handed in. Teachers should also let students know who they will be working with within the class. The teacher should also ensure that all equipment is working correctly and that students can access whatever they need during class time.

The teacher can decide on a "quiet signal" to let the class know when to begin working. This can help children who are always disruptive early in the morning. It can also serve as a reminder for students who tend to be loud and disruptive during class time. Teachers should show their students how they should take turns, and share with them how much participation is required from them during class time. They should be able to move through the day while working with their peers and teachers.

Teachers must also make sure that their students know what is expected of them. They can use visual cues to help shape behavior. These may include a picture of a student getting ready for school, a student with his backpack by his desk, or sitting at her desk waiting for class to begin. This will help students regulate their behavior since they will see what is expected of them at each point in the day.

Understanding the Child's Point of View

Children with ADHD may be confused by classroom procedures and can become easily disappointed when they don't understand what they are supposed to do. Teachers must ready themselves to deal with the child's frustration, as it is common for children with ADHD to act out when they don't understand what is happening.

• Confidence building

Children with ADHD often feel out of place in class due to their inability to pay attention for long periods. The teacher must be aware that this is common in children with ADHD and approach them kindly, encouraging them and building their confidence.

• Behaviors that are not learning-related

Teachers must approach children with ADHD with patience and understanding. When teachers see that the behavior is not related to the lesson, they should approach it with patience and teach important lessons that apply to the child's everyday life. This can help build the child's confidence, and also help them realize they don't have to act in certain ways in order for people to accept them.

• It's not a matter of intelligence

Children with ADHD often seem intelligent outside of their classroom environment. However, they often find it hard to focus on classwork and may take the easy route when attempting a solution or forming a response. Taking the easy route means people may not see the child's true potential. The teacher should recognize this and be patient with this behavior.

• Love for learning

Children with ADHD must be encouraged to live up to their potential and be proud of what they accomplish. The teacher must approach the child with respect and kindness, telling them how proud they are of them for attempting to complete schoolwork, even though they can't stay focused for very long periods.

• Punishment

Teachers must realize that children with ADHD may act out over small frustrations, especially when they cannot finish work on time or don't understand why certain things are happening. The teacher must approach this with patience and build the child's confidence rather than punish them for acting out.

CHAPTER 9: SUPPORTING YOUR CHILD'S NEEDS WITH ADHD

Parents of a child with ADHD can help improve the child's school performance by advocating for her. This advocacy may take many forms, from working with other parents to change district policies to meeting with a teacher or school staff member to discuss problems and potential solutions. Parents who are highly involved in their child's education and actively advocate for their child may provide critical assistance to teachers and school personnel working with students with ADHD.

One of the most vital reasons for parents to be involved is that they can provide essential information to teachers and others about how their child learns, what she needs from the classroom environment, or how she responds best to certain demands or situations. Parents can help teachers and school personnel by educating them about the characteristics of ADHD. Parents should provide information on the multiple reasons children with ADHD behave as they do, as this will help teachers understand why the child's behaviors are problematic.

Parents who provide teachers with adequate information about their child's learning style and accommodations can make all the difference in determining what type of classroom environment will best benefit their child. This is best done with the help of a professional experienced in working with students with ADHD.

Sometimes, parents need to ask fundamental questions about what is expected of their child in the classroom. Many parents need information on how to help their child with organizational skills or set realistic goals for their child while in school. Some simple suggestions may be more effective than others when working with students who have ADHD.

Parents can provide effective advocacy if they discuss these issues directly with teachers and work on problem solving together, if possible. Parents can also communicate with their child's teacher to ensure that the accommodations listed in the child's IEP are adequate and appropriate for his current needs. Some parents may choose to use a note from their child's doctor to provide information about the child's ADHD to the school.

Parents may also want to consider attending school council meetings when policies are being discussed regarding students with ADHD. Parents should speak up if they think a specific procedure is not in their child's best interest. They can also advocate for other resources their child might need in the classroom, such as a computer or sound-reducing headphones. By supporting staff at these meetings, parents can help their child get the extra help and resources he needs to succeed in school.

Parents can be advocates for their child with ADHD by meeting regularly with teachers or the school administrator to discuss their child's progress. Parents can also communicate with their child's teacher to help make any changes in the classroom necessary to improve the child's performance. This may include changing seating arrangements or altering an assignment given to a student with ADHD.

Parents can make a change in their child's life by becoming highly involved in the process of education and advocating for their children. A parent's advocacy may be crucial in influencing a teacher to change a classroom setting to improve the child's behavior. Parents supporting their children may also help when problems arise in school or when changes need to be made with grading or classroom rules.

Many schools have counselors who are there to provide suggestions on what kind of help the student needs. A counselor is a good resource, but it is essential to not expect too much from them. They have limited time and may have to do paperwork that will take away from the individualized help you are looking for.

Advocacy, of course, is not always easy for parents to do. At times, it can be frustrating and overwhelming for anyone who has a child with ADHD to work with the educational system. However, parents should never forget that it is important to be proactive about their child's education. Parents engaged in advocating for their children will provide critical assistance to teachers and school personnel trying to assist ADHD students in reaching their full potential.

Attacking Developmental Problems

Many parents are afraid that their children with ADHD are not developing properly due to the disorder's symptoms. However, parents need to understand that many factors can affect a child's development, including behavioral, emotional, and cognitive symptoms beyond lack of focus or impulsivity. While ADHD can contribute to developmental delays, children with ADHD who receive appropriate counseling and staff training will not be affected as negatively as those who do not.

The American Academy of Pediatrics (AAP) recognizes that not all children with ADHD will exhibit developmental delay, and it urges physicians to be aware of this aspect of childhood disorders. The AAP also encourages physicians to educate their patients about the possible co-morbidities that may occur with ADHD and encourage parents to seek professional assistance if they believe that their child is showing signs of developmental delays.

The Virginia Department of Education has endorsed the use of appropriate screenings to identify children with ADHD who may be at risk for developmental delays. The Virginia Department of Education also supports appropriate assessments that may help determine if developmental delays are present. These screenings can be made by personnel trained to use them, such as school psychologists, teachers, counselors, and school nurses.

Parents should discuss concerns regarding their child's development with their physician or the appropriate school personnel so they can refer the child for an assessment if necessary. Parents can also ensure that these professionals are updated with current research on ADHD and its co-morbidities. These professionals may be able to provide parents with specific suggestions regarding interventions that may help their children.

Effective interventions include developmental programs, such as a community-based preschool program or a Head Start program. Parents should inquire about special education services in the public school system and advocate for their children to receive appropriate assessments and supports from qualified professionals. It is equally important that parents understand what type of intervention is being provided to their child to monitor whether or not it is helping significantly. This can help them determine if the intervention should be modified in any way or if additional services are needed.

Parents should also be familiar with their school district's extension services, which may include the services of a family counselor, social worker, or psychologist. Parents should discuss what types of interventions they believe will benefit their children in school and at home. These professionals can be useful when it comes to finding out what kind of interventions would work best for their child.

In addition, parents can ask their loved ones for help in monitoring their children with ADHD. In addition to this, they can take advantage of technologies that can monitor their children's progress with developmental skills by using a web camera or a digital recorder. Seeing and hearing your child's daily activities can be very helpful when it comes to identifying whether or not the child is advancing correctly. This may result in a better understanding of what interventions will work effectively for your loved one with ADHD.

Specialized counseling and educational interventions may also be recommended for those who exhibit developmental delays due to ADHD due to the co-morbidities that occur as more than just behavior problems.

As you can see, parents can take on an extremely important role in educating teachers, school personnel, and even their child's peers about ADHD. Finding strategies that work for both the child and the teacher will help improve education for everyone involved.

Developing Your Child's Practical Communication Skills

Research has shown that effective communication is essential for any family. Of all the vital skills children learn as they age, listening skills are arguably the most important. Studies have shown that listening is critical for children's cognitive development. You can demonstrate to your child how to listen by having conversations about your day together. When children learn through demonstration, it is easier to explain the concepts, and they become more permanent in their lives.

When you first learn about ADHD, it may seem like a huge hurdle that needs to be overcome. However, as parents learn how to manage their frustrations and the struggles they face daily, they will start gaining new perspectives on parenting that can help them develop more effective strategies for dealing with their child's ADHD symptoms. Still, many of these issues cannot be fixed without professional assistance from a therapist or psychiatrist.

Raising a child with ADHD can be challenging, but parents can mitigate the effects of the disorder if they are willing to learn about it and accept that their child will not grow out of it. Parents may need professional help to ensure that their child's needs are being met, and must take on a parenting role conducive to raising a child with ADHD.

Parents who have children with ADHD should consider learning about the problem from medical professionals who treat it regularly. This will help them identify any development problems and assist their child to develop coping mechanisms to manage their symptoms.

Parents should also learn about the strengths and weaknesses that ADHD entails. Parents can then recognize their child's unique abilities. For example, a parent who notices that her child is very responsible may build her child's confidence by giving her more responsibilities.

Many parents of children with ADHD choose to hire outside caregivers for their children. These individuals may be able to help them learn how to manage their child's ADHD needs. To increase the likelihood of positive outcomes, parents should develop a close relationship with these professionals so they can develop strategies geared towards improving communication between themselves and their children. Professionals can provide effective intervention strategies, both at home and in school settings, so children receive the treatment they need.

A pediatrician may have a greater insight into the possible benefits of medication in a young child with ADHD than a clinician typically does in an adult patient. Clinicians are also able to discuss possible side effects that may occur with certain medications. A physician can also help parents learn about the possible causes of ADHD and ways to address them. Effective, direct communication between parents and physicians will increase the likelihood of a positive outcome regarding treatment options.

A physician may also encourage the parent to have their child evaluated by a mental health professional. Parents may want to contact a mental health professional specializing in treating childhood psychiatric problems, such as a child psychologist or social worker, when their child's behavior affects the family's daily functioning.

Bringing a Psychiatrist into the Classroom

It can be challenging to bring a psychiatrist into the school to diagnose ADHD, but it is possible. Parents may find that the process is worth it, as it can help teachers and parents better understand and address their child's needs.

A psychiatrist who specializes in ADHD may offer multiple treatments for children with the disorder. These might include medication, cognitive behavioral therapy, or a combination of both. In addition to these options, a psychiatrist might recommend counseling or tutoring as well as educational assessments. He or she may also recommend parenting classes for those with young children.

Psychiatrists who specialize in ADHD have likely studied the disorder from various angles over years of research and practice. If your child's teacher or school administrator is reluctant to work with a psychiatrist, ask them why. This discussion may be enough to change his mind or at least raise awareness about ADHD and its impact on the classroom.

Even if an administrator is not willing to bring in a psychiatrist, another option for parents is to take their child for an evaluation at a nearby medical facility that serves as an official diagnosis center. Check with your state government to see if any exist within your area. The school system may help cover these costs, particularly if teachers are concerned about your child's behavior.

PART 4 - FRIENDSHIPS AND ATTENTION DEFICIT HYPERACTIVITY DISORDER

CHAPTER 10: THE IMPACT OF ADHD ON FRIENDSHIPS

C hildren that suffer from ADHD are more likely to have problems connecting with peers, making friends, and participating in social activities. But they can make friends. However, in order to form friendships, some children with ADHD may need extra support and time to learn the skills that enable them to relate to others. They may also need more support than other children as they may be perceived as uncooperative or disruptive. The social skills they learn enable them to participate better in peer activities and contribute socially to groups of peers.

Inspire your child to partake in sports or other activities, giving them a chance to make friends with other kids with similar activities. If they have trouble finding a group with the same interest, you might want to find a coach or other adults who can help them find a group of kids who share their interests.

Talking to other adults or coaches about your child's ADHD can help them become more aware of their behavior. This will help them know how to treat your child, and with help the child feel good when interacting with others.

If your child's ADHD causes too many difficulties in forming good relationships, they must be given more emotional support. Talk to your physician about medicines specifically formulated to help children with ADHD learn social skills. These types of drugs are called sub-therapeutic, wherein medication levels are lower than necessary for treating ADHD. These lower doses can provide benefits without causing side effects.

The medication can be raised gradually by adjusting the dosages until it reaches therapeutic levels for treating ADHD. Ask your physician about the possible side effects of the medication to provide your child with a good balance in emotions and social interactions.

A common problem experienced by people with ADHD is that their minds tend to wander away from the conversation, causing them to miss vital information. It is more difficult for them to develop good friendships and relationships, a problem that often persists throughout their lives.

They can also be taught about body language that indicates someone is paying attention. This includes avoiding things such as looking around when talking with people, being distracted by noises, looking down when listening to someone talk, and fidgeting or twitching while listening to someone. It is also essential for them to pay attention to what other people do and how they respond, in order to learn more about appropriate social interactions.

Children with ADHD may not be as popular as other children because of their apparent lack of interest in certain things. They will tend to be less socially adept than other children, making it difficult to form relationships.

Your child must learn how to respond appropriately when addressing others. They can learn how to calm themselves down and manage their emotions to feel better and handle these situations more effectively.

Social Skills Training

Some children with ADHD do better in group activities than in solo activities. Others do better if left to themselves. If your child is attending school, you can also look for opportunities for them to form friendships outside of the school setting.

Learn how to support your child during social interactions. You may need tools, such as books or tapes on social skills, that you can give your child before certain events.

Talk to your child about what you expect of them. Be clear about how to act in social situations. Make sure that your child knows if they are doing well or not doing well.

By helping them learn how to control their ADHD, you can help them develop good social skills that will result in making friends and participating more fully in class.

ADHD's impact on friendship development is universal. Sufferers struggle with the processes that allow them to be outgoing and comfortable in social situations. The student may be labeled as "quiet" or "reluctant" by their peers, leading to other negative feedback like teasing and bullying.

Most of the time, ADHD children struggle with an inner image of not being bright enough or good enough compared to their friends. They are often the last to be asked to join in on games or invited to parties. When they are, it is often reluctantly. For parents, this can be difficult because it sometimes feels like you are failing your child when they don't fit in with their peer group.

Society is quick to label children who do not fit in well with peers as "bullies" or "troublemakers," which only reinforces the ADHD child's behavior and self-image.

ADHD children are more likely to use their hyperactive behavior as a defense mechanism due to feeling very overwhelmed by their social surroundings. This can lead to social situations becoming increasingly worse. When an ADHD child feels threatened, they are less likely to listen to others, and because of this, they are much more likely to respond aggressively to a real or perceived threat.

A great way to prevent your child from becoming a bully is to give them virtues to live by and share how important it is for them to do the right thing. When they understand the potential negative impact of their actions, they are more likely to listen and follow through with your requests. By giving them this kind of support, they will see themselves in a positive light, which will build up their self-esteem that can lead to stronger friendships later on in life.

If your child seems to be in a downward spiral, try talking with them about what is stressing them out. Often, when things get too much, they do not have the courage to speak with you about it. Your child must realize that you are available for support in dealing with their problems. This will help build their confidence to become more open and honest in sharing difficulties or conflicts with you and others.

It can be confusing for your child when the other kids are teasing them about being "different." Teasing can lead to self-doubt and feelings of isolation, making it much more difficult for a child to respond effectively. Talk to them about this issue, so they understand that being different is okay. It is okay to be yourself, even when other people do not understand or accept who you are. This will help them deal with peer pressure more effectively, and help them feel more confident in addressing their differences with others. It is imperative for family members to be supportive in helping kids with ADHD become more outgoing and participate more readily in social situations.

The most common difficulty reported by parents of children with ADHD is the child's tendency to be aggressive with peers or siblings (83% of parents). Parents also noted that these children were overly competitive (47%), had difficulty following directions (45%), had trouble getting along with other children (40%), and made immature fashion choices (40%).

Rather than reacting with aggression, your child needs to understand that there are better ways of dealing with difficult situations. Tell your child that they can stand up, speak their minds, and be themselves even if they do not necessarily fit in with other kids. They also should not fear expressing themselves, as long as they do so in a respectful way. Encourage your children to tell you if somebody is bothering or teasing them so that you can intervene on their behalf.

If your child has gotten into an argument, make sure that the incident is discussed openly and honestly between you and your child. Determine if any extenuating circumstances may have led to the fight. Talk with your child about dealing with the situation in the future so that they do not resort to fighting again. By understanding what led them to fight in the first place, you can help alleviate much of the frustration before it results in a physical confrontation.

Children with ADHD are more likely to experience pain during playtime or physical activity due to frequent accidents, irritability, worry, and tiring quickly. They are also more likely to be wounded during play because of their hyperactive behavior, leading them into dangerous situations without realizing it.

When it comes to ADHD, the most common sources of pain are other children who are overly rough, bullying by other children, playing in unsafe situations, not hearing what is said, using poor judgment when talking to other children, losing interest in playtime quickly, overactivity while doing tasks or activities and being unaware of feelings.

Some parents have found that taking the time to teach their child beforehand about avoiding injury while playing can be helpful. This includes written instructions on preparing themselves for the activity and what to do if they feel pain.

Be sure to avoid excessive roughhousing, which can easily lead to injury. Instead, encourage your child to focus on activities that will give them a sense of accomplishment.

Have your child show you how they play during playtime so that you can inform other family members and children of the behaviors they should avoid if they want to have a safe time. As a result, your child with ADHD might get teased less and experience less peer pressure.

Encourage your child to make all efforts to get ready for physical activities in order to avoid painful accidents and injuries.

How ADHD Affects Friendships

Many parents of children with ADHD feel that their child's relationship with their peers is very complex, as social interactions are often a source of both joy and pain for these kids. You can usually tell if your child is struggling with friendships when they become anxious, upset, sad, or even angry about what happened during a social interaction. They may also feel guilty or embarrassed about things that occurred during a social encounter.

Some children with ADHD tend to regularly go on social media sites like Facebook, Twitter, and Instagram. They may even maintain secret social media accounts to look for friends online as they have problems making friends in person and often feel isolated.

There are many differences in friendships that you can expect for your child with ADHD.

A common sign of friendship problems is if your child is being bullied by peers during their interactions. Your child may become withdrawn and isolated from their peer group and seem like they prefer to be alone.

Motivate your child to spend time with friends in person rather than online or by text message, which can leading to misunderstandings. The same is true for using the phone, although sometimes texting can serve as a social outlet for your child by helping them connect with friends in different places.

Make sure your child is not engaging in negative peer interactions by talking down to others, mocking others, or demanding that others listen to their opinions. Doing so could lead other children to dislike them.

Your child may be seeking out friendships with children who are mean, disrespectful, or difficult to be around. Encourage them to cultivate friendships with kids who are kinder or more respectful of them. Motivate your child to make friends with people they can talk to about their ADHD and how it affects their life.

Many parents have found it helpful to discuss their child's condition with their friends' parents. By doing so, they can gain a better understanding of what causes certain reactions in their child in a social setting. This way, parents can better understand their child's behavior, can treat it accordingly and can talk to them about what is going on.

Help your child set up a social media profile if they wish to do so, but inform them that you will be monitoring it regularly to prevent any cyberbullying.

As discussed above, some children with ADHD may be teased by their peers because their ADHD makes it difficult for them to interact socially with others. Teasing is usually an attempt to gain power over the other person. Teasing may involve making fun of another child's appearance or intelligence, taunting, mocking them about something they can't do, mocking their names or characteristics, insulting other people publicly (such as on social media), threatening physical harm (e.g., "If you do that to me I will beat you up") or verbal harm (e.g., calling someone fat, ugly or stupid), and ignoring them.

Teasing can make your child feel inferior and give them an opportunity to compare themselves to others. It may also make them believe they are not worth much, which can make them feel sad, anxious, angry, insecure about their personal identity, depressed, and/or hopeless. It can lead to low self-esteem and discourage social interactions with peers.

One strategy that can help children with ADHD to cope with teasing is to name the child's behavior when they feel teased, such as "That reminds me of when Mom told me to stop doing that, and I didn't listen and then look what happened. That's how I feel right now."

If your child is being teased, they should tell the person that they are not interested in their negative or critical opinions of them. Tell your child that they do not have to allow anybody to make them feel bad about themselves, especially if their comments concern something about which they cannot control (ADHD).

It is also good for your child to learn how to ask other kids to stop teasing them if they are being teased because of their ADHD. If your child tells the person who is teasing them not to do it again, it should be done in a compassionate but firm tone. It may be necessary for you to help your child with this strategy.

Teasing can lead to depression, anxiety, low self-esteem, difficulty sleeping, poor concentration, and low self-confidence. Teasing may have adverse effects on your child's physical health as well. Children may be less likely to participate in sports because the activities require them to interact with others, which can be difficult for them to do.

Teasing can also lead to an increase in your child's ADHD symptoms. For example, suppose your child is being teased about their ADHD. They may feel upset about the teasing, uncomfortable in social situations, less likely to concentrate on schoolwork or chores, or less interested in learning new information or activities. A child with ADHD may become more aggressive towards their peers when they are being teased because they are angry about the taunting. They may also become more anxious about what other people think of them.

Teasing can also make your child less likely to ask for help when they need it. If your child is being teased about their ADHD, they may learn to avoid friends who make them feel bad. They may also drop activities in which they are being made to feel bad about themselves. If the activity is something that they enjoy or that helps them reduce their attention problems, then stopping can perpetuate their attention issues.

Children with ADHD may feel disconnected from other children because they don't want to ask people to make fun of them. This can cause a sense of isolation.

Teasing can also cause a child with ADHD to become aggressive or violent against their peers. When a child with ADHD is made fun of, they may respond by saying mean things about the person doing the teasing. Sometimes this response is because they think the comment about their ADHD is true, and they want to defend themselves against it. This can result in a power struggle between two children that can cause additional problems, such as fights or arguments that upset other kids who are around them.

Making fun of people because of their ADHD, especially children, is considered offensive by the majority of parents. In a 2016 study, 98% of parents felt that teasing a child for having ADHD was wrong. In the same study, 81% said they would tell the person to stop if they saw this happening. Teasing a person with ADHD can lead to social isolation for your child, which can make it harder for them to improve on their attention problems.

The Good Morning Institute (GMI) is a nonprofit organization based in Tempe, Arizona, that works to prevent bullying among children ages 5–18. It was founded in 2004 by Richard Leventhal, then president of the Association for Childhood Education International (ACEI), and Peggy O'Neill.

The GMI runs the anti-bullying campaign "Stop Bullying Speak Up" by encouraging children to speak up if they are being bullied, rather than letting the bullying behavior continue, and has created a list of "dos and do nots" to help parents prevent bullying. The organization's website states that its purpose is to collect data on the prevalence of bullying and ways to stop it.

Similarly, the ADHD Foundation supports those with ADHD, their families, and professionals. It works toward raising awareness about ADHD issues and supporting children with the disorder. The group provides information on ADHD-specific medications, treatments, and other relevant information about the disorder. It also runs a blog for parents titled "ADHD Foundation Blog." Founded in 2006 by Joel Nigg, the organization is based in Oregon.

How ADHD Affects Socializing

As we have learned, children that suffer from ADHD can have a hard time making and keeping friends. These children often refrain from doing things that help others get to know them, such as participating in discussions or paying attention to what others are saying or doing. They may also take longer than other kids to respond when someone is talking to them. Sometimes they may not pay attention because they are thinking about something else, such as getting home to watch television. Children with ADHD can be hyperactive and impulsive. They may interrupt others while they're talking or do things without considering how the person around them will feel (such as telling secrets).

Children with ADHD can also have trouble getting along with friends because of their delayed reaction times and poor organization skills. For example, if a friend wants to play a game of baseball and your child doesn't know how to play, he or she will be left out and ignored. Sometimes these children are excluded by the other kids because they don't want to play with someone who is so different.

In order to make friends, some children with ADHD may try to seem cool. This can result in them engaging in risky behavior or doing things that are dangerous. To attract attention, these children may show off or act out while playing sports. These kinds of behaviors can make it more difficult to form a friendship with a child who is not similar to them.

Because they have a hard time understanding people's feelings, children with ADHD may not be able to tell if others are being serious or joking. For example, if someone says something that is offensive, the child with ADHD may not understand that it is wrong. Because of this, making fun of others can seem like a normal thing for them, if no one corrects them. This may cause your child to make fun of people who do not want to be made fun of and who could hurt your child physically or emotionally as a result.

Disagreements and arguments among children with ADHD can cause them to lose self-control. This can lead to tantrums and fights that harm relationships. These fights can cause other kids to be mean, and can lead people to dislike your child.

Children with ADHD may not understand how to work well with others. Some children experience issues when they're in a group, and they don't know how to follow directions or when they should be doing/saying something. They don't know to wait until there's a pause in the conversation to speak up. Children might feel like their problems are more important than other people's problems. They might also think they are the only person with problems. This can make them feel upset or misunderstood.

Because of these issues, children with ADHD often have trouble making friends they can confide in. This can make it very challenging for them to get through challenges in life, such as the loss of a family member or moving to a new house or city.

Children with ADHD can be impulsive and hyperactive, causing them to immediately say the first thing that comes to mind, even if it hurts someone else's feelings. This can lead children to get into fights and arguments with other kids who don't want to play with them because they hurt others' feelings just by being around them.

How ADHD Affects Quality of Life

Children with ADHD have trouble thinking about the future, so it is hard for them to plan ahead. They also have trouble remembering the past, so they are not good at remembering details about their lives or even what happened just a short time ago. That can make it hard for them to be successful at school or in social situations. Children with ADHD may have difficulty having fun because they don't pay attention to what other people are doing around them. This can make it challenging for them to enjoy playing games or having fun outdoors. They may also hurt themselves, which can make their parents feel bad and can lead to more behavioral problems in their children.

These problems can make it difficult for children to make friends, attend school, or do their chores. They may also suffer from unhappiness and feelings of loneliness. Children with ADHD often have poor self-esteem because they do not understand how to be happy. This can lead them to feel worthless.

CHAPTER 11: ASSISTING YOUR CHILD IN BUILDING FRIENDSHIPS

I t's no secret that living with ADHD can be difficult for the child and their family. The child with ADHD often struggles to make friends because children with ADHD often don't follow the social norms. Children who are not delighted with their lives may also shy away from adults they do not know well, preferring to trust kids they already know.

Children may also resist adult authority figures like teachers and parents because these adults don't always seem to understand them. Children who are bullied can find solace in schoolmates who share similar interests; however, they may find themselves excluded from groups of kids who are more normal-looking than them.

As you watch your child learn to navigate friendships, it is crucial for you as the parent to be an active participant in this process. Even the most well-laid plans and best social skills can be derailed by a parent who makes negative comments. A lack of support creates withdrawals in the friendship group or intervenes in a way that sabotages your child's efforts to form friendships.

As your child prepares to make friends, you need to learn about their strengths and weaknesses. It would help if you also analyzed their strengths and weaknesses concerning the other children in the class. You need to understand how these strengths and weaknesses affect the social status of your child.

For example, some children with ADHD are great talkers and can get other people fascinated by their stories, experiences, and adventures. Some children with ADHD may stand out in class by wearing more attractive clothes than others or having more advanced athletic skills. Sometimes this is because they have parents who are willing to spend time with them practicing these skills. Other times it is just because of natural talent.

You need to understand your child's strengths and weaknesses before beginning the training process. If you need help, consult with the school social worker, a parenting education specialist, or other professionals trained to work with children.

You don't want your child to become angry at themselves or others because of their ADHD symptoms. Your child must develop friendships without an ongoing conflict between them and other kids in the class.

Watch how your child relates to the other kids in class and then analyze the strengths and weaknesses of your child in relation to these other children. It is difficult for some parents to accept that their child may be different from others and may not fit in with them and their friends. This can lead to significant stress and unhappiness for the family. Parents need to learn how to identify and respect the differences between their children and others.

Teach your child about social skills and how they are used in different social situations. You must lead by example on this issue. When you are home, let your child observe how you relate to other adults, kids, pets, etc. Your actions will send powerful messages about what makes for good relationship skills. Remember, you are your child's role model. If you are unsure about how to act around other people, get help.

Your child will be more successful in building friendships if you do these things:

- Be sure to introduce the child to others. The more practice your child has with socializing, the better it will be for your relationship with your child. If your child has siblings at home, let them know that your son or daughter has ADHD and that this makes it difficult for the children to learn social skills. However, you don't want them to be rude or dismissive of their brother or sister's difficulties.

- Encourage your child to spend time with peers and adults who can help them learn social skills. This will allow the child to practice and improve their social skills, skills that will make them more successful in school and more popular throughout their life.

- Don't let errors in communication continue without correction. Never allow your child to get away with not keeping track of what is said by others. Try not to become rigid and set in your ways; accommodate your child's needs if they make a communication error.

- Don't comment on how hard it is for your son or daughter in class so that it appears that you are being critical of their ADHD behavior. Let them know that it takes a lot of effort for them to stay focused in the classroom, which is why they may make errors.

- Don't make unfair judgments about your child's social behavior. Try not to point out how they seem different from children who are not suffering from ADHD.

If you are critical, your child will feel defensive and withdrawn from you.

- Tell your child that there is nothing wrong with being different from their peers.

- If your son or daughter struggles to relate with other children, try to identify the problems in the relationship. Often, there is a misunderstanding between the two children involved in a friendship conflict. If so, help your child find ways to resolve the problem.

- Teach your child how to listen and watch for cues from others in the classroom setting, and how not to become frustrated when they do not know what is being asked of them by their teacher or other adults in their class environment.

- Model social skills by leading by example. Make sure you spend plenty of time with your child to establish a positive relationship at home.

- Remember that, at any age, it is not uncommon for children with ADHD to have adjustment problems in school. These can lead to failure in many aspects of life if they are not correctly identified and treated early on in the process.

- Tell your child that they can tell you about their day at school if they encounter difficult things there.

- Remember that your child needs acceptance and support from you to deal with this problem, not criticism and rejection.

- If you feel the need to point out their errors in communication with others, use a matter-of-fact tone of voice as if you were talking about the weather or something as commonplace as the color of a wall or piece of furniture.

- Watch for signs that your child is getting angry or frustrated.

- Teach your child some ways to calm themselves down when they get angry or frustrated, like deep breathing exercises, counting to ten slowly, listening to some soothing music, or making funny faces in the mirror.

- Encourage your child to play games that require them to work with other children. Some games that encourage this type of interaction are Legos, board games, cards, and sports.

- Never ignore aggressive behavior on the part of your child unless it is necessary for you or someone else's safety. If so, explain why you are doing it even if they get upset.

- Never shout or scream at your child for making mistakes in social situations. Your child will feel very uncomfortable if you do this.

- Teach your child to tell you about any trouble they are having in school.

- If your child has problems with a peer, try to be a mediator and not the judge. Get the two children involved in talking about how they feel and let them make their own decisions in order to solve the problem.

Things your child can do to build friendships

Playing sports

Sports are one of the best ways for children to interact because they provide a unified goal, a team mentality, and cooperation between individuals. Sports give children the opportunity to feel a sense of belonging and to work together as a group.

Although it is not true of all kids with ADHD, most like sports and play them. However, their lack of attention can negatively affect their performance in various athletic endeavors. Problems with organization and time management also may affect their performance in the game.

Before trying out for a team or joining the practice, here are some strategies that can help your child to excel in their game:

- Make sure that they consistently exhibit good sportsmanship. This means they should always applaud the other team, limit trash-talking or taunting of any kind, and avoid controversial topics.

- Identify your child's strengths so they can be put to best use in the game. For example, if your child is a strong runner, they might be used to make a play when the other team rushes the ball in a certain part of the field. When your child knows their strengths, they can use them to the best of their ability.

- Help your child to become aware of their weaknesses and how to overcome them. For example, if they lack good running skills, they can work on developing better directional skills. Although this might not directly change how fast your child, it will improve their ability to run using their peripheral vision.

- Set up a schedule for practice and stick with it. This way, your child will know what to expect and may work on their weaknesses more effectively.

When scheduling practices, give your child a chance to have a friend join them. If the buddy is not playing with your child, they can still coach them to improve their skills. For example, suppose your child is having problems controlling their emotions. Encourage them to learn more about mental relaxation exercises like counting backward from 100 by moving their hands over their eyes before starting the training.

- Pay attention to the other children on the team because this will help your child feel more comfortable around others at the practice who are also "different." This can set your child up for success in more ways than one. For example, if another player on the team is doing well, they may tell your child how to improve their skills and help them see the positive things they can do. Your child will become a more valuable asset to the team and play a more critical role in their game by listening and improving their skills.

Playdates

Many parents might think they can help their child find friends by setting up playdates; however, this is not always the best practice. There is learning that needs to be done in social settings with people close in age who like the same things as your son or daughter. Some people may not want to attend a playdate because they do not like the child. If this is the case, parents should try to find a different friend for their child, who is more suitable.

Teach your son or daughter about appropriate greetings and saying "bye" when they leave a playdate. They should also learn to ask someone if they want to play a game or do something for a while.

Your child may not be good at making friends right away. But they will eventually learn from their mistakes and can try again later. Your child will generally outgrow their social and personality problems as they get older and will learn over time which kids to meet with.

If your child is rejected by someone they want to be friends with, you can ask them why they were denied. If they make another friend, make sure they understand how important it is to keep their new friend's confidence. This will help your child have more friends in the future.

How and When to Tell Your Child They Have ADHD.

There are different ways for you to tell your child that they have ADHD. When considering how to tell them, it is important to consider your child's age and what is going on in their life. Most parents prefer to wait until their kids are older before they tell them that they have ADHD. You can also wait until they go through a significant change in their life, such as a new school or are expecting a new sibling.

When telling your child about ADHD, make sure you let them know what it means and why it affects them this way. This will help your child feel as though they have a voice and that you understand their needs.

Make sure that you give them opportunities to ask you questions. This will let them know that they can come to you when they need help with something.

There are different ways you can tell your child about having ADHD. You can tell them verbally or through written materials like articles or books. Many kids like to read articles and books about ADHD, so this is another way for you to help them learn about the condition without feeling overwhelmed. This also allows them to ask their questions when they are ready instead of forcing them to address them if they do not want to right away.

How you tell your child about having ADHD is a personal decision. It is essential to choose a way that will fit your family's situation the best. Make sure that you tell them how it can influence their life and why they might struggle with specific situations. Keep in mind that they might be more receptive to learning about their condition if they are not pressured into talking about it right away. Make sure they understand that you will be there for them if they need support.

When telling your child about having ADHD, it is important to let them know that they do not have to take medication if they do not want to. Do not force your child to take medication if they struggle with the side effects. Let them know that there are other ways to cope and manage their symptoms.

When your child goes through a significant change in their life, such as a new school or a new sibling, it is a good time to tell them about their ADHD. If they are going to a new school with a different curriculum, let them know they might struggle, but encourage them to try hard and ask for help if needed. Knowing that you will be there for them when they need it is also important.

Some parents prefer to wait until their kids are older before discussing their condition with them. However, some may prefer to discuss the condition when their children are at a younger age so they can better manage their symptoms. One thing to keep in mind is that some kids have a hard time discussing or even thinking about their ADHD until they are older. Whatever you choose, it is important to let them know you will always be there for them if they need support.

Tell your child how the disorder affects them and why they might struggle with particular situations. If they are going to a new school or they have a new sibling on the way, let them know that it might be more difficult for them to adjust compared to other kids, but that you will always be there for them if they need help.

For those without ADHD themselves, learning about having ADHD is frequently a matter of perspective. In some cases, the knowledge comes from observing the symptoms of those in our lives who have ADHD. Very often, our perspective of those who have ADHD is limited by what we observe in others and media rather than by actual experience.

Helping your Child Find the Right Friends

Finding the right group of friends for your child to talk to is a good way for them to have a supportive group of people to discuss their struggles with. This will help them feel more comfortable discussing their symptoms with others, knowing that they are not the only ones struggling.

Their peers may also be able to offer useful tips or coping techniques on how to manage their symptoms. If they are struggling with something, it is always good for them to talk about what is bothering them with one of their friends. Have your child's friends come over to your house so he can talk about his issues in a comfortable environment where he feels safe, and can open up without being worried that anyone will judge him. This will give him the ability to let out what he is feeling while also feeling safe. If you do not have friends that your child can talk to, find them a network of people that they can talk with online.

How to Get Your Child to Let Go of a Friendship

Getting your child to let go of a friendship can be hard because losing a friend can be very painful. Tell your child that it is important for them to listen to what their friends have to say and that letting go should not be completely based on them but also on what their friends want. However, always mind that your child does not have to let go of a friendship if they think there is still some good in it.

It is important to remember that sometimes friendships will end naturally because kids grow at different rates, or because there are no longer things in common between the two friends. If your child is having trouble letting go of a friendship, they can always call their friend and ask them if they would like to continue with the friendship. This way, it can be a mutual decision, and your child will not feel so much pressure to let go of the friendship. Remind your child that they should always be respectful and kind to their friends.

Explain to your child that sometimes things do not work out between two people. Friendships change and sometimes people grow apart as they age.

Explain to your child that some people might be popular in school, but that does not mean they are the best person for them to be friends with. Some people spend all of their time trying to be attractive or being liked by others. People who are popular in school might seem good at first, but if they are not kind or do not value meaningful friendships, they may not be worth being friends with.

It is important for kids with ADHD to have the right group of friends because this will help them feel less worried about being accepted or fitting in with others. When kids have friendships with others who share similar interests, they will be able to feel more comfortable being themselves.

Explain to your child that people are allowed to have different opinions about things and that it is okay to not agree with other people. This will help them realize that the opinions of others are not the be all and end all.

Help your child understand that now is their time to be happy and enjoy themselves without worrying about getting into trouble or what other people might think. They are allowed to have different feelings from others; feelings that may even change from one day to the next because they are growing up.

CHAPTER 12: INFORMING FRIENDS' PARENTS

When your child with ADHD has friends, you will need to inform their parents about the condition so they can understand what is going on with your child. This is also vital because it helps other children and adults understand why your child might react inappropriately in different situations.

Not all parents will be quick to come around to the idea that their child's friend has ADHD. Some might feel as though there is nothing wrong with their child, so there should be nothing wrong with yours either. When talking with these parents, it is important to be patient and understanding. Let them know that even though keeping their child in a small social world might seem like a great idea at the time, it cannot work in the long run.

When educating friends' parents about ADHD, make sure that both you and your child are there to talk with them. This will make it more personal and relatable for both your child and the other child's parents.

Keep yourself calm when talking about your child's condition. This will help you and the other child's parents understand what is going on with your child and why they act out in certain situations. Allow them to see your child as a normal kid who just happens to have ADHD.

Your child's ADHD symptoms may seem different when they are with their friend's parents compared to when they are around you. Keep in mind that these symptoms may differ because of your child's different environments. Explain to these friends' parents what your child's symptoms might be, so they know what to do when they see your child.

Make sure you have a good relationship with these friends' parents because this is how these friendships will stay stable. You and your child can set up play dates and activities that they can do together. This will allow you to keep the friendships going strong.

The activities you choose can vary depending on the kids, but it is helpful to ask your child's friends' what they would like to do with your child. This can help you set up specific games and events that will benefit your child and their friend.

Setting up age-appropriate events helps the other child's parents understand how your child interacts during these activities, and any challenges that are likely to arise. It can also help explain to these parents that the way a child acts is not always a replication of how they feel inside.

You and your child must make sure that these friendships stay strong by setting up activities together as much as possible. This will also help your child feel as though they are not alone in their struggles. It will also help your child understand the challenges of making friends, and to appreciate the friends they do have.

The Importance of Effective Communication

Communicating with your child's peers is a difficult task that many parents have a hard time doing. Identifying what is going on in your child's life and verbally communicating the challenges of having ADHD is critical in helping them open up and relate with their peers better. Communicating with others will help your child build stronger relationships with their peers.

Identifying and teaching appropriate behaviors is an important part of communication. You may not be able to talk to the other parents specifically about ADHD, but you can talk to them about behaving appropriately in certain situations. Effective communication can also help your child avoid misunderstandings they might have with their peers, which will help them avoid feeling out of place and isolated from the group.

Now that you know some of the best ways to communicate effectively with your child's peers and their parents, it is time to put these skills into practice. Whether your child is starting a new school or they have known their friends and parents for a while, it is essential to effectively communicate with them so they can understand how ADHD affects you both. Identifying what it means to have ADHD will help make sure that everyone involved understands what the condition means in real life. Communicating effectively with these peers and their parents will help give you and your child a chance at making stronger relationships.

Using the "Teach-Back" Technique

The "teach-back" technique is a very helpful skill if you are trying to communicate effectively with your child. It is an effective tool that you can use with your child when they are having difficulties communicating with their peers. It is also another great way for you and the other parents to effectively communicate about ADHD.

This technique encourages you and other parents to give feedback about what it means that your child has ADHD. Remember that each child will have their own challenges when it comes to communicating with their peers. Your task is to find ways to work around these challenges so the other parents can give feedback about how they see your child behave or react in certain situations. You can do this so there is little to no confrontation, but you still get the point across in a helpful way.

Before you decide to use this technique, there are some things that you should consider. These include the age of the other child, the age of their parents, and how you are feeling about your child's behavior. You should also consider what you want to say to the other parent, what your child may have difficulty understanding, and how you are going to express yourself. Taking these things into account will help you determine the best place for you to teach-back.

Now you have decided to use this technique, it is time for you to learn some tips on how to successfully use this tool.

1. Focus on the "hot spot."

The "hot spot" is the part of the situation that you are focusing on for this interaction. You may be using this interaction to communicate with your child, or you might be using it to communicate with the other parents. Either way, you need to focus on one specific aspect of your child's behavior before trying to teach them how to improve it. This way, they have a chance at making the right decision every time they are in that situation.

2. Explain the situation and find a solution.

When you and the other parent agree that your child is not handling the situation correctly, you should try to understand why they are having a difficult time. This can be accomplished by understanding what your child does in this situation and how it affects their peers. For example, if your child does not communicate when they need to, you can figure out what your child is doing in this situation when they do not communicate well. Once you have identified when your child does not communicate well, you can try to communicate with them, so they can recognize when this happens. This will help them know how to react when they are in this situation again in the future.

3. Keep going until you find a solution.

This technique may take several attempts before you find a solution that works for your child and their peers. However, the chances of finding a solution that works for everyone will increase if you keep trying. You do not have to be a part of the interaction to teach-back. You can stay away from the situation and still use the "teach-back" technique.

4. Keep going until everyone is satisfied with the solution.

Making sure that all of the people involved agree with the solution will help ensure that no one feels as if they are being treated unfairly. You may have a solution to the situation that works well for you and your child, but it does not work well for the other parents. If the other parents would like to add their input into this interaction, then you can add that into your solution.

5. Teach-back only what you want to say.

It is important that you do not teach-back additional information or lies that will make the situation worse. This is one of the best ways to make sure that you are staying on track with what your main point is. It will also keep you from getting frustrated with the conversation or with other parents. You may even want to teach-back what the other parent said about what your child does.

6. Make sure everyone's needs are met.

Making sure that everyone has their challenges met in the interaction will help make this technique work effectively for everyone involved. You do not have to be part of this interaction. The child and the other parents can still use this technique, which will make it possible for everyone involved to find a solution that works well. This will make the interaction go smoother and prevent conflicts from occurring in the future.

Using the "teach-back" technique is a great way to make sure that all of the people involved in an ADHD-related situation are satisfied with how it was handled. It can also be very helpful when your child is having difficulty communicating with their peers.

You have learned how to use the "teach-back" technique. Now it is time for you to apply what you have learned. You do not need to go to a group meeting or tell another parent that they are doing something wrong. Instead, practice this technique by having conversations with your child about what he does at school or during other activities. Remember that the goal is to teach them how to communicate so they can prevent problems from happening in the future.

After practicing this technique for a while, it will become second nature. The more you practice, the better that you will get at using it and finding solutions that work for everyone involved. Keep practicing this technique with your child periodically. This will help you make sure that your child is handling their behavior problems appropriately.

Putting the "Teach-Back" Technique into Practice

Now that you know how to use the "teach-back" technique in conversations with your child or other parents, it is time to put it into practice. You can use this technique whenever your child is having trouble communicating with their peers. This will help get them to learn how they are communicating incorrectly and how they can improve in future.

1. Figure out what the main issue of your conversation is.

First, consider what the main problem is that your child is having with their peers. If you think they are not communicating when they need to, then you can start by asking them what they want to communicate. Once you know the main issue of the conversation, then you can start learning how to improve this communication.

2. Look for another parent who does not have ADHD to involve in the conversation.

Whenever you want to use the "teach-back" technique, look for another parent who does not have ADHD to involve in the conversation. The other parent should also be able to help your child with communication or other issues that they are having throughout the day.

3. Have a conversation with the other parent about what your child needs to do.

Have a conversation with this parent about what they can do to assist your child with their challenges. You can also chat with your child's teacher or another adult who interacts with him throughout the day and in order to gain their thoughts and feedback.

4. Use the "teach-back" technique until everyone is satisfied with the solution.

When you have a conversation with the other parent or teacher, ask them what they think your child needs to do or say during an interaction. You can use this same process for your child as well. If the other parent gives you great ideas about how your child should respond, then ask them to teach-back their ideas so that your child can understand what they need to do in a situation.

5. Agree with the other parent about what your child needs to do.

Once you and the other parent agree on what your child needs to do during an interaction, you can go back to your child and ask them if they still feel like they need to say or do something differently, or if they are happy with the solution reached. Be ready to talk with them about this solution so they can decide on whether or not they will use it in the future. Remember that this step does not necessarily mean that your child will know exactly what they should do or say, but it will get them to be more aware of the different ways that they could respond to their peers. This will help them have a better understanding of how others communicate and how they can be more effective in these relationships.

6. Talk with the other parent about what you did or did not like about the conversation.

Make sure you are honest about how you feel. This will help the other parent know whether or not they need to do something different in the future. If what they did was good, then tell them so, in order to strengthen your relationship.

7. Have a talk with your child about what they learned during the conversation.

This will help your child understand that they need to do differently if they want to be successful.

8. Repeat the process until the conversation is successful.

Continue using this technique until the conversation is effective. After your child has had enough practice with this technique, they will be able to notice when something does not go well, and will be able to change things for the better.

The "teach-back" technique is an easy way to help your child improve their interactions with their peers. It can be used with anyone who does not have ADHD. However, it is important that you use this at the right times so that your child can become comfortable with it and really learn how to communicate well with others. If you use the "teach-back" technique at the right times, your child will continue to take advantage of it as they grow older and will make more friends.

When Not to Use the "Teach-Back" Technique

There are some instances when you should not use the "teach-back" technique. For example, it can also be difficult for your child to use the technique when they are not with you or another adult. If you are not around to help them use the technique, your child may have trouble knowing what to say or do if they interact with their friends. Instead, you can give them instructions for something like having an appropriate conversation with one of their close friends at school. This will help them feel more comfortable being around others.

PART 5 - FROM ADHD TO ADULTHOOD

CHAPTER 13: GROWTH MINDSET: ACHIEVING GOALS AND REACHING TRIUMPH

What we teach our children shapes the way they think and the goals they achieve throughout their life. This is no less true for our children with ADHD. If we want to help them achieve success in life, we must teach them to believe in their potential.

A growth mindset teaches children that intelligence can be improved through hard work. It makes them see mistakes not as signs of failure but as opportunities to learn more about what works and why. It helps children see a struggle as a way to get better at something rather than a reason to give up.

A growth mindset gives them scruples and a passion for acquiring new skills. This can have a positive impact on their development and on the development of their confidence in the future. If we want our children who suffer from ADHD to believe in themselves, we need to teach them how to make mistakes and learn from them. This means not only encouraging them when they succeed but also helping them try again when they fail or make mistakes. This is important because most people stop trying if they fail or make mistakes too many times in a row. They give up instead of trying again.

Mistakes are normal and a part of learning. It's important for children to understand that if they cannot get something right in one attempt, it does not mean that there is no chance for them to learn it at all.

A growth mindset is all about helping children harness the power of effort and believe that their effort can lead them to succeed if they work hard enough. Children with ADHD may feel that learning new things will never come easy to them. But if they put in the hard work necessary, they may be able to discover new skills or knowledge.

Transitioning to Adulthood

Knowing what to expect in adolescence can help us prepare for the long road ahead.

This is especially true for our children with ADHD, who will need all the help they can get as they transition into adulthood. After all, the transition into adulthood is no easy feat for anyone.

However, for children with ADHD, it can be even more difficult. They may find it hard to cope with changes both in their environment and in their thought processes. Adolescence is a time where we feel like we can take on the world and face any challenge. But with ADHD and the subsequent behavioral problems, sufferers may find it difficult to do. They may start to question who they are and who they want to be. This is also the time when they will begin to experience all the demands and responsibilities of adulthood, such as keeping up with school, having job and family responsibilities, and taking on all the challenges that come with newfound freedom. So how can we help them transition successfully into adulthood?

It may be helpful to talk to them about what this time in their life means and how it will differ from other stages in their life. It is also helpful for them to know that you do not expect them to become different people just because they are transitioning into adulthood. Rather, they should know that you want them to develop into the best versions of themselves. Adolescence can be hard for anyone and your child may experience difficulties during this time. But he might also experience some positive changes in his behavior too.

There are some things that you can do to help your son or daughter successfully navigate through adolescence. These include:

- Help them develop a social circle and build positive relationships through school, work, and extracurricular activities.

- Encourage them to make better decisions and to challenge themselves in their studies and work.

- Teach them about finance and to prepare for job opportunities.

- Have them meet with a physician to assess their needs and plan for treatment so that they can best prepare for adulthood.

- Ensure they have some time to spend at home with their family.

- Help them find ways to relax and unwind or exercise in order to release some of the anxiety they may be feeling.

- Give them space for their interests, hobbies, and new

passions without pressuring them into being perfect or completing tasks on the spot.

Ultimately, you want your child to know how to navigate the challenging times of adolescence. This process may feel overwhelming for them, but it will also encourage them to become more responsible adults with life skills. Although they may not be able to turn these challenges into achievements yet, it is important that they learn the skills that will help them reach their goals in adulthood. The longer they can spend in adolescence, the better they will be able to handle the demands of graduate school, a good job, marriage, family life, and parenthood.

It is important that you talk to your child about this time in their life. To help your child understand this stage in their life, talk with them about being a teenager and what it means to be an adult. It may also be helpful for them to watch a movie, read a book, or listen to a podcast so that they can learn more about this stage of life.

Often people advise their children not to dwell too much on the difficulties they may be experiencing because it will only make things worse. But everyone has emotional ups and downs, and these feelings are very normal and rarely cause damage.

If you are troubled about your child's progress during this time, remember that it is never too late to have them evaluated.

Evaluation can help guide them toward treatment and can help them catch up on some of their developmental needs. If you are concerned about your child's problems with impulsivity and hyperactivity during this time, there may be options for treatment, such as medication or working with a clinical counselor to help them deal with their challenges.

CHAPTER 14: PROSPECTS FOR ADHD IN THE FUTURE

The outlook for children with ADHD has been improving as we understand more about the condition and how to live and cope with it. If we look at the past half-century, we find that we have made a lot of progress in developing education and treatment options for ADHD and its behavioral and learning challenges.

It is important that we continue this trend and work even harder to understand ADHD in order to develop more effective and accessible treatment options. This is especially important for children with ADHD, who need every opportunity we can give them in order to succeed in life. It is vital that we continue to do our part in improving the quality of life for people with ADHD.

One of the things we can do for families is to provide adequate training to the professionals who support them. This will help them make more knowledgeable decisions about treatment options, how best to teach, coach, or supervise these clients, and how best to care for their needs.

Parents should expect that they will need guidance in learning how they can live with ADHD more effectively (e.g., how to create order, structure, and regularity in their lives to avoid unnecessary stressors). They should also expect that they will need support in knowing how they can provide the best care for their children. No one should face ADHD alone.

It is important that those professionals who provide this ongoing training and support be carefully selected based on their demonstrated knowledge of ADHD. Professionals should also be regularly monitored on the basis of their ability to meet the needs of those with ADHD properly. This will help them develop more effective ways to teach living successfully with ADHD, which will then help more people learn to live well with the condition.

The quality of treatment must be addressed as a matter of urgency. We know a lot about treatment options, but still more is needed to improve the quality of care and to develop affordable, widely available options for all families. Many children with ADHD never receive help at all – but without help, they never learn to cope as well as they could.

Another important goal for the future is improving our understanding of how schools can best take care of those students who have been diagnosed with ADHD. We all want the best for these children, and we should be working together to make sure that schools provide them with what they need – both for their own benefit and that of their classmates as well.

Another big area of concern is the way we work to prevent ADHD in the first place. Here, we need to think carefully about how we can identify and address the environment that makes ADHD likely to develop. This is best done by more research on environmental factors that could play a role in ADHD in children. We need to learn more about how to create an environment that supports children in becoming happy, motivated, confident individuals who are successful. By better understanding how these environments affect individual development, we gain a much bigger picture of ways in which things can be better for everyone.

Over time, researchers have learned a great deal about ADHD and about the critical role of the environment in development. If we apply what this knowledge has taught us, it is possible that future generations could see the disorder disappear altogether.

If we can learn how to promote positive mental health in children, it could have multiple benefits for all children. The resulting generation of well-adjusted, responsible individuals could result in a safer, more peaceful world. If we can help all children develop into strong and capable minds, then everyone benefits – including people with ADHD, who will then be able to succeed without any special considerations.

Of course, it is not just children who would benefit. Everyone who lives in a world filled with people who think clearly, act with confidence, and are motivated to reach their full potential will reap the rewards. A world without ADHD may be a world where everyone can thrive.

It is vital that we stay on progress with our efforts to understand the disease, develop effective treatment options, and offer ongoing support for all those living with ADHD and their loved ones. We may not yet know what lies at the end of this path, but it offers limitless possibilities for all who choose to follow it.

People with ADHD need all the support and guidance we can give them so they can lead wholesome, healthy, and productive lives. They will need ongoing training and support from those who know how to provide it best. In doing so, everyone with ADHD will have an even better chance of living a full life that is characterized by success, happiness, and contentment.

CONCLUSION

According to a national survey run in 2021, more than one-third of parents of children with ADHD worry about the adverse effects of the disorder on their children's happiness, confidence, and success in life. Luckily, if you know what to look out for, ADHD can be very manageable.

A child with ADHD is more than just "quirky." It can cause significant damage to them if left unchecked. The frustrating part is that most cases of work-related stress, depression, and even substance abuse are directly related to ADHD.

Children with ADHD need constant supervision and management, including monitoring their diets, daily routines, and peer-to-peer relationships. Always remember that you are the voice for your child. If you don't speak up on their behalf, then nobody else will either.

To avoid the worries, frustrations, and busloads of tears that are breeding within your child, you need to understand what it takes to ensure their happiness and success.

Understanding the condition better with best enable you to help your child with ADHD. There are many ways that ADHD affects a child. Not knowing what having ADHD means can lead to devastating consequences for you and your child, but knowing the condition will improve not only your own life but your child's life as well. The critical thing to remember is that ADHD is not something that you or your child did, but something that happens to both of you. It's also not something you can outgrow; it is an illness with no easy solutions. If left untreated, ADHD will continue to plague your child until they come to terms with what it means and take steps to deal with it.

Knowing how to communicate with others will improve both your and your child's lives so you can focus on the most important things. It is important to remember that no matter what your child is going through, there will always be someone to help you and your child when they need it the most.

Many professionals offer techniques and treatment methods that can help with all kinds of different situations that people who have the condition may encounter. It is not as much a condition as it is a lifestyle. There are several ways to help your child with ADHD, but you need to consider that there will be roadblocks to overcome along the way.

ADHD is a severe disorder that can negatively affect how a person lives their life from the time they are young through to adulthood. The main thing people with ADHD need to realize is that they are not alone. There will always be people who will want to help you and your child, but you must first open up and be willing to ask for assistance. While this might be difficult at first, it definitely can be done.

It's important for people who have the condition to learn how to communicate better with others in order to express themselves and to get the help they need.

The bottom line is, if people are willing to work with you and your child, there will always be a way to overcome your struggles. Always remember that your child with ADHD needs support in more ways than one. You must support them by being the voice of reason when they feel they have none. Stand in their corner when times get tough. Be there for them when they don't want to go through all the hardships of having ADHD. They need someone who can lead them by example, not by merely telling them what needs to get done, but by showing them how it's done. Work with your child and their school to provide the necessary help and support. Don't let them think they're alone in their struggle. Be there for them and educate them on how to get through any situation they're faced with. Talk to other people who have experienced these same struggles so you can get some much-needed perspective, not only from someone who has been in your shoes but from someone who has been through the same adversities and come out the other side even stronger.